T0123789

Be a Leader Not a Ruler

Helpful Advice for
Music Ministry Leaders

Jeff Bishop

WESTBOW
PRESS®
A DIVISION OF THOMAS NELSON
& ZONDERVAN

Copyright © 2021 Jeff Bishop.

All rights reserved. No part of this book may be used or reproduced by any means, graphic, electronic, or mechanical, including photocopying, recording, taping or by any information storage retrieval system without the written permission of the author except in the case of brief quotations embodied in critical articles and reviews.

This book is a work of non-fiction. Unless otherwise noted, the author and the publisher make no explicit guarantees as to the accuracy of the information contained in this book and in some cases, names of people and places have been altered to protect their privacy.

WestBow Press books may be ordered through booksellers or by contacting:

WestBow Press
A Division of Thomas Nelson & Zondervan
1663 Liberty Drive
Bloomington, IN 47403
www.westbowpress.com
844-714-3454

Because of the dynamic nature of the Internet, any web addresses or links contained in this book may have changed since publication and may no longer be valid. The views expressed in this work are solely those of the author and do not necessarily reflect the views of the publisher, and the publisher hereby disclaims any responsibility for them.

Any people depicted in stock imagery provided by Getty Images are models, and such images are being used for illustrative purposes only. Certain stock imagery © Getty Images.

ISBN: 978-1-6642-2852-8 (sc)
ISBN: 978-1-6642-2853-5 (hc)
ISBN: 978-1-6642-2851-1 (e)

Library of Congress Control Number: 2021906094

Print information available on the last page.

WestBow Press rev. date: 03/25/2021

Scripture quotations taken from The Holy Bible, New International Version® NIV® Copyright © 1973 1978 1984 2011 by Biblica, Inc. TM. Used by permission. All rights reserved worldwide.

Scripture taken from the New King James Version® Copyright © 1982 by Thomas Nelson. Used by permission. All rights reserved.

Scripture taken from the NEW AMERICAN STANDARD BIBLE®, Copyright © 1960, 1962, 1963, 1968, 1971, 1972, 1973, 1975, 1977, 1995 by The Lockman Foundation. Used by permission. www.lockman.org

Scripture taken from the Contemporary English Version © 1991, 1992, 1995 by American Bible Society. Used by Permission.

Scripture taken from the King James Version of the Bible.

Scripture quotations marked (NLT) are taken from the Holy Bible, New Living Translation, copyright ©1996, 2004, 2015 by Tyndale House Foundation. Used by permission of Tyndale House Publishers, a Division of Tyndale House Ministries, Carol Stream, Illinois 60188. All rights reserved.

Scripture quotations are from the ESV® Bible (The Holy Bible, English Standard Version®), copyright © 2001 by Crossway, a publishing ministry of Good News Publishers. Used by permission. All rights reserved.

Scripture quotations marked (GNT) are from the Good News Translation in Today's English Version- Second Edition Copyright © 1992 by American Bible Society. Used by Permission.

Scripture taken from The Message. Copyright © 1993, 1994, 1995, 1996, 2000, 2001, 2002. Used by permission of NavPress Publishing Group.

Scripture taken from the Modern English Version. Copyright © 2014 by Military Bible Association. Used by permission. All rights reserved.

Scriptures taken from the Complete Jewish Bible. Copyright © 1998 by Messianic Jewish Publishers and Resources. Used by permission.

Scripture taken from the Holy Bible: International Standard Version®. Copyright © 1996-forever by The ISV Foundation. ALL RIGHTS RESERVED INTERNATIONALLY. Used by permission.

[Scripture quotations are] from the Revised Standard Version of the Bible, copyright © 1946, 1952, and 1971 the Division of Christian Education of the National Council of the Churches of Christ in the United States of America. Used by permission. All rights reserved.

Scripture taken from The Voice™. Copyright © 2008 by Ecclesia Bible Society. Used by permission. All rights reserved.

A thought provoking look at where we
go wrong as ministry leaders.
A true eye-opener and must read for all church leaders.
After all, we are all leaders.

Let no unwholesome word proceed from your mouth, but only
such a word as is good for edification according to the need
of the moment, so that it will give grace to those who hear.
—Ephesians 4:29 (NASB)

Contents

Acknowledgments

I would like to begin by saying thank you to WestBow Press for making this book a reality. Thank you Matt Dahl for calling me to get the ball rolling just minutes after submitting my application. Thank you Hanna Nate and Leandra Drummy for coordinating this project. Thank you Caleb Ritchey, Danielle B. and the editorial department for all you hard work. Thank you Bob De Groff and the design department. I was unable to get everybody's names, so thank you to everyone who helped on this project. You all did a fantastic job.

You had no jacket or hat, yet you stood in the pouring rain to pray for me. Thank you, John Cunsolo. You are a true shepherd.

Thank you to my mentors and role models: Chuck Lowey, Pastor Christophe and Elizabeth Akagla, Glenn and Sheri Rigby, Charley and Joan Leggase, and Esther Ette.

Thank you to my brothers and sisters in leadership: Alfredo and Judy Bortolotti, Jeff Wiesner, Fabiano Bussolaro, Jonatas Azevedo, Louise Ryan, Sean Spooner, Josh Doucette, Craig Langlois, Barbara Feldsdstein, Dan D'Amato, Glaubert Carvalho, Derick, Watts, Brian and Sandy Douglas, Paula Cuneo, Nancy Campos, Chris Tighe, Barbara Tosti, Uli Kane, Diogo Silva, Herman and Gretchen Fuller, Bethany Franklin, Alan and Michelle Brunson, John and Lorri Dudley, Heather Sacharewitz, Linda Baker, Devon Seymour, Jhonathan Morais, Dominic Luoni, Silverio Da Silva, and Andy Maddocks.

While serving on quite a few different ministries throughout the Church, I've had the privilege to serve with so many great people. In fact, there are so many of you that it could possibly take an entire chapter to name you all. Thank you to all my brothers and sisters in Christ; I'm sure you all know who you are. You're all awesome friends. Thank you for your love, prayers, and support.

I also can't forget to say thank you, Mom, for putting up with all the noise and letting us rehearse in your basement with our Marshall Stacks and Ampeg SVTs, vibrating the entire house and causing all your knickknacks to fall off the shelves. Then after all that, you still came to every gig. Thank you, Mom. I love you.

Thank You, God, for always being with me, even when I didn't know You were there. Looking back on my life, I can see now where You pulled me through the toughest of times.

Thank You, Holy Spirit, for guiding me and keeping me on the straight and narrow path and for filling me with Your fruits.

You are a King, yet You don't rule us from a throne or wear a royal robe. You walk among us shoulder to shoulder, dressed as a shepherd, and lead us by Your example. You didn't come for us to serve You. You came to serve us. You don't demand that we bow at Your feet. Instead, You wash ours. You've never once told us to submit to You, though we do anyway.

You were beaten, mocked, and scorned for us. You poured Your blood, Your sweat, and Your tears out or us. You took upon Your shoulders every sin of the world, for us. You hung on a cross and died a criminal's death for us. You battled death and darkness in the grave and won for us. You rose to life again in victory for us. You returned to Your home in Heaven to make a way for us. And because You gave everything You have to us and for us, we now can come home to be with You forever.

You are our Shepherd, and You are our King forever.
Thank You, Jesus.
Amen.

> *in everything give thanks; for this is the*
> *will of God in Christ Jesus for you.*
> *—1 Thessalonians 5:18 (NKJV)*

Introduction

In my entire life, I never considered the possibility of writing a book, but the idea came to me one day, and I got right on it.

I was serving with a music ministry at a Christian church in Massachusetts when a situation arose that I knew I couldn't handle by myself, so I turned to two of our pastors for help. I was seriously considering filing a formal complaint, so I typed it out and gave each of them a copy to review. I didn't sign it, nor did I put my name on it. I only wanted their feedback and suggestions for a way to resolve the issue without drawing any attention to it.

I suspected that either way we went with it, there would be a meeting of some sort, in which I would be asked to speak, so I began formulating a speech in my mind. I was driving to work while talking to myself and rehearsing different approaches and ideas. I didn't want it to be accusatory, negative, or demeaning in any way, so I was choosing all my words carefully. And the more I talked, the more ideas filled my mind. I started to recall service messages, training sessions, devotionals, books, and, most important, Scriptures. The ideas became so abundant that I began dividing them into categories and was planning to type them out so I could pick and choose what to save and what to toss in an effort to keep it as short as possible, but the ideas just kept pouring in.

As I continued talking it out, I began listening to my own voice as though I were listening to a training instructor. I then began thinking that what I was hearing really wasn't half-bad advice, so I started paying closer attention to what I was saying and realized that I was actually learning something from it all. I knew right there and then that it was the Holy Spirit speaking through me, and He was indeed trying to teach me something.

Then on one occasion, while I was walking my dog, Kira, around the backyard and talking my way through more ideas, another idea came to mind: I should use all these ideas to write a book. Then the floodgates just seemed to open right up. Titles for chapters began coming to mind. I thought about what material I would put in each one, along with which Scriptures to go with them. And then the next thing you know, "Old Jed's a millionaire" (*The Beverly Hillbillies*). Just kidding. The Oldies radio station in Boston, which is no longer active, had a trivia game, and one of the questions was "What's the next thing you know?" Well, that's another story for another day, but now you know the answer. So anyway, the next thing you know, I'm sitting here writing this book. I hope you enjoy reading it. But I also hope you get something out of it.

Trust in the LORD with all your heart And do not lean on your own understanding. In all your ways acknowledge Him, And He will make your paths straight.
—*Proverbs 3:5–6 (NASB)*

We go through the motions and "do church" by habit rather than by the Living One spontaneously moving in and through us. We have programs and policies that take on a life of their own, slowly marginalizing the Jesus who birthed the church to begin with. If we aren't careful, the church becomes an impersonal organization rather than a living organism.
—Chris Tiegreen

CHAPTER 1

———— ✥ ————

Know Their Story

The sheep know their shepherd's voice. He calls each of them
by name and leads them out. When he has led out all of his
sheep, he walks in front of them, and they follow, because
they know his voice. The sheep will not follow strangers.
They don't recognize a stranger's voice, and they run away.
—*John 10:3-5 (CEV)*

This chapter was inspired by two pastors who ministered a small-group leader training session. I wanted to begin here because my big take-away from that session was to know the stories of our group members. I believe this is an important aspect of leadership because it will help us to understand our group or team members' needs.

Even though that training session was for small-group leaders, the same principle can certainly apply to leading in music or other ministries as well. You don't need to know every detail of people's lives, but knowing your members' stories can be helpful in many ways.

Strengths and Weaknesses

The New England Patriots won Super Bowl LIII, which made them the best football team in the world. Julian Edelman was voted most valuable player of the game, which made him the best football player in the world. He achieved that award by playing the position of wide receiver. Now get this—when the Patriots drafted him, he was a college quarterback. So how does Coach Bill Belichick know to use him as a receiver? He knows his story.

Coach Belichick could have released Edelman as a result of his ineffectiveness as a potential NFL quarterback. But instead, he found Julian's strengths and used them to help the team win. Can you imagine how many players could have been released because of weaknesses? But instead, Coach Belichick focuses on the players' strengths and builds game plans around them. And by doing so, the Patriots have made it to the Super Bowl nine times in his nineteen years as their head coach, and they won six of them. That's not a bad record when you consider there are teams that have never made it to the big game—like the Detroit Lions, for example, and they have been in the league since 1930.

My point is that if Coach Belichick wasted time focusing on the players' weaknesses, he may have been watching the Super Bowl from the comfort of his living room.

Focusing on the strengths of musicians and vocalists will have similar advantages. For example, you may have a song you would like to add, but it has a fairly complicated drum part. So you leave the song out or perhaps resort to simplifying it, and it never sounds quite right. Now imagine how helpful it would be to know that one of the drummers on the team used to play for a Rush tribute band. Anybody who is familiar with Neil Peart's playing knows what I am getting at here. This means you have a drummer who can play virtually anything, so let's break it down a little.

Weaknesses

Right off the bat, the negativity of the word *weakness* should be a red flag because God would never put anything negative into our thoughts. Therefore, it must be coming from the enemy. And as positive as it may sound on the surface, looking for weaknesses to improve upon in team members can be hurtful, condescending, and insulting, not to mention evil. Yes, evil. As we know all too well, the devil is very clever, and he will stop at nothing to try to thwart us. He knows that he can't take away our salvation and that he can't avoid his eternal damnation, but if he can keep us from bringing others to Christ, he has won a small victory. You may ask, "How would that apply here?"

He plants ideas in your head and makes you believe they're your own so you look for areas of improvement and sit people down to talk to them about it. You may do so in a kind and loving manner, yet you're unwittingly attacking their confidence because then they may begin to doubt the things they do well. And it can become an uphill battle for them from there. If that happens, they can feel unworthy and believe that they don't have the ability to bring others into God's Kingdom. In other words, the devil is working through you to glorify his own kingdom.

Be alert and of sober mind. Your enemy the devil prowls around like a roaring lion looking for someone to devour.
—1 Peter 5:8 (NIV)

In 2 Corinthians 10:5 (NIV), Paul says, "We demolish arguments and every pretension that sets itself up against the knowledge of God, and we take captive every thought to make it obedient to Christ." So how do we do that? I like the way Paul puts it in Philippians 4:8–9 (NIV); he says,

> Finally, brothers and sisters, whatever is true, whatever is noble, whatever is right, whatever is pure, whatever is lovely, whatever is admirable— if anything is excellent or praiseworthy—think about such things. Whatever you have learned or received or heard from me, or seen in me— put it into practice. And the God of peace will be with you.

I don't know about you, but that sounds pretty positive to me, which brings us to the flip side of this.

Strengths

As a leader of any church, ministry, or team, it's our responsibility to build up and edify the members who look up to us, which is why it is so important to look for and focus on their strengths. When you sit someone down and talk about what he or she does well, it makes that person feel more confident in his or her abilities. And the more confident people feel, the quicker they will grow. In fact, this will even help their weaknesses improve faster because they will begin to believe they can overcome them. Now that's God at work and not the enemy.

I can do all things through Christ who strengthens me.
—Philippians 4:13 (NKJV)

Witch Hunt

During the seventeenth century, many innocent people worldwide were being tried, tortured, and executed based on accusations they were performing witchcraft, and a great deal of those horrors took place right here in Massachusetts in the town of Salem. Paranoia broke out, and any questionable behavior drew attention and false accusations. In fact, one case resulted from a trivial argument between two neighbors. So, needless to say, it got out of hand. And as horrible as it was, the history remains and draws many tourists to Salem, especially each year around Halloween.

You may be wondering why I brought this up. Well, I really don't want to beat this to death, but I cannot stress strongly enough how important it is to be careful when you're looking for ways to make improvements. Because intentionally looking for a team member's weaknesses is very much like, you guessed it, *a witch hunt*, and it is sometimes referred to as "witch-hunt mentality."

So it's really quite simple. Dismiss any thought that has any negativity at all, regardless of how harmless it might seem, because it can only be coming from one place, the evil enemy. Focus only on positive thoughts and ideas. There's not really much more that needs to be said here. So always remember that weaknesses come from Satan, and strengths come from God.

"I am the good shepherd; I know my
sheep and my sheep know me—
—John 10:14 (NIV)

Be a Reader

I'm not talking about reading books or documents of any kind. I'm talking about reading people. You don't need to be an expert at it, but knowing a few of the basics can help. There are quite a few good books available that can help, including *How to Read a Person Like a Book* by Gerald I. Nierenberg and Henry H. Calero. One thing I would suggest is to watch for signs of lack of confidence. This is very important for leaders. Because, as leaders, it is our responsibility to edify team members. A few basic things to watch for are nervous smiles, droopy shoulders or slouching, and a change in voice pitch (quieter and deeper).

These can possibly indicate low self-esteem but are not always 100 percent accurate. It's best to have a baseline for a person's normal behavior and watch for sudden changes.

A good example I can give took place while I was attending band leader training. We were working on music qualifiers—which is where the leader or a vocalist will speak to the congregation. He or she will pray, explain the church music to newcomers, and welcome them to sing along. One of the members of our group, let's call her Jane, needed coaxing to do hers. She did do a good one, but she had no confidence in what she did. One of the leaders gave her what I thought was excellent practical advice, but Jane still had a nervous smile and drooping shoulders.

So when the leader left the room, one of the other members, who we'll call Jack, spoke to her. He didn't say anything to her about how to speak publicly or how to deliver a qualifier because what Jane needed went much deeper than that. She needed spiritual help, so Jack told her that she's a child of God and reminded her how much God loves her; that He would never plant negative thoughts in her head; that negative thoughts only come from the enemy; how to take authority over negative thoughts through what Christ did for us; and that if the negative thoughts keep coming back, she should just ignore them because they are nothing but lies.

As Jack was speaking, I watched Jane's face fill with joy and her shoulders puff up with confidence. And the following week, Jane, with her newfound confidence, was selected to give a music qualifier with a microphone on a lighted stage in front of approximately a dozen of us. She came out and gave one of the best music qualifiers I have ever heard.

God was definitely working through Jack that day to help him recognize that another member needed spiritual help. He will always speak through us if we open ourselves up to Him. And by quoting Scripture and directing people to the Bible, that's exactly what we're doing. There's nothing wrong with practical advice as long as we know when to use it so people don't take it to mean that they are not good enough. A true shepherd, however, or a true leader will recognize whether our team members need practical or spiritual help.

So, What's Their Story?

When we come to Christ, one of the first things we learn is that we need to humble ourselves, and that's not always easy to do because we are still conditioned by our many worldly living habits. As Dr. Neil T. Anderson has said, "We do not have an instant delete button." For instance, you may have a member who never felt the need to humble him- or herself before and isn't too sure how to, so he or she simply doesn't talk about his or her experience for fear of sounding boastful. As admirable as that may sound, it could possibly hold that person back from reaching his or her full potential as a contributing team member. In some cases, people could be holding something back from you that could be an extremely valuable resource for the team, like an instrument needed for a special presentation. In smaller churches, it's easier for a leader to get to know the team members on a personal level, but that may not always be possible, especially if you are leading for a church with multiple campuses and a fairly large team. Sure, you see all the team members fairly frequently. You know their names, their vocal range, and what instrument they play. But how much do you really know about them?

> *through knowledge its rooms are filled*
> *with rare and beautiful treasures.*
> —*Proverbs 24:4 (NIV)*

Hidden Treasures

You may already employ a similar approach, but when conducting auditions, gather additional information on the members' applications, such as the following:

- What other instruments do they play?
- Do they have other helpful experience (technical or otherwise)?
- Do they also sing (if auditioning for a specific instrument)?
- Do they teach music in any capacity?

Those are just a few examples, but I think you get the idea. And even if you already do this, how much of that information do you remember down the road? It's also difficult to keep track of who plays what when you have a team of any size. And let's face it, with all the other responsibilities and duties we tend to, stuff like that probably almost never crosses our minds.

You may have other creative ways of gathering information, and that's good too, but still, it's difficult to keep track of it all, so try to employ ways of reviewing it and keeping it fresh and accessible for future use. One way to do this could be to delegate leaders for each instrument. A guitarist could be assigned to getting to know the other guitarists and a drummer the other drummers and so on and so forth. Once again, you can create your own way of doing this, but the point I'm getting at is, follow up on it, and don't let valuable information get swept under the rug.

It's not necessary to know every detail of their personal lives, like so-and-so grew up in Herkimer, New York, or the new drummer goes to Stop and Shop whenever there's a sale on Friendly's ice cream, but knowing more about their musical and theatrical experience could prove to be very helpful. For example, suppose you discover that the team has several members who play stringed instruments, such as violins, cellos, and double bass, just to name a few. There also just happen to be some members who can play brass instruments. Now you have the makings of a small orchestra.

You could then invite them in from time to time just to highlight certain parts of specific songs or for special presentations. And I know that with all our modern technology in place, we have many of these instruments right at our fingertips with Abelton, Playback, or whatever system we may be using at the time. But how cool would it be to have somebody playing the instruments live once in a while? The possibilities could be endless.

And to top it off, you could be adding a whole new boatload of fun for the band. I know we need to focus on the why and not the how. But we are human, and by nature, we have a secret desire for church music to be fun. If you deny that, you're only kidding yourself, but we'll get into that in a later chapter.

Now imagine this: It's Christmas Eve, and you begin "Joy to the World" with a tubular bell intro. Did that get your attention? Well, it really is quite simple for almost anybody to play. It's all eight notes in order going down any major scale. And if it's in the key of C, it's all on the lower row of bells, which is the equivalent of the white keys on the piano. How easy is that?

Sorry, I didn't mean to get into a music lesson there, but by now you must be wondering, *Where are we going to get a set of tubular bells?* You could rent them, but it might be expensive. And even if you wanted to, not too many places have them available. But what if there is somebody on the team who plays chromatic percussion? And what if that person also just happens to have orchestra bells, crotales, a Burma bell, wind chimes, temple blocks, timbales, melodic cow bells, triangles, a gong, and a Chinese bell tree? Oh yeah, I almost forgot about the tubular bells. After all, doesn't everybody have a set of tubular bells in their basement?

> *And they made bells of pure gold,*
> *—Exodus 39:25 (KJV)*

> The bell tolls for thee...
> —Neil Peart

CHAPTER 2

―― ❧ ――

If It Ain't Broken

Whatever is good and perfect is a gift coming down to us from God our Father, who created all the lights in the heavens. He never changes or casts a shifting shadow.
—James 1:17 (NLT)

One thing I could never understand is why somebody would buy a perfectly good house, in move-in condition, and completely gut the place before moving in. I always feel like asking, "If you didn't like the house, then why did you buy it in the first place?" They end up spending almost as much as the purchase price for the remodeling. So in effect, they're buying the house twice. I don't know. Maybe it's just me, but it just doesn't seem to make much sense.

When I was preparing to move back to Holliston, Massachusetts, which is where I grew up, after looking at a few houses I thought I would like, I ended up buying the one I didn't think I was going to like. As it turned out, the only thing I didn't like about it was that it didn't have a garage for my Harley, so I just got a very large shed to solve that problem. People can be pretty funny too. They're always offering remodeling advice, like tear out this wall and open it up, or rip out the cabinets and get something modern. The thing is I like the floor plan and old cabinets. They're part of the appeal that drew me to make an offer in the first place.

I don't want to waste a lot of time here on house buying, but I just wanted to add that this house has the original kitchen cabinets from when the house was built, and they're still in good shape. I know. I can already see the eye rolls, but hear me out. This house was built back in the days when carpenters measured, cut, built, and finished the cabinets right on-site to custom fit, and with real wood no less. So if you really think for one second that I'm going to go to Home Depot and buy prefabricated cabinets made from that fall-a-particle board with scribes for one-size-fits-all installation, yeah sure, I'll get right on it (eye roll).

> *Generations come and generations go,*
> *but the earth never changes.*
> *—Ecclesiastes 1:4 (NLT)*

New Assignment

After years of serving on the music ministry for the church you attend, the long-running team leader steps down, and you get the call to step in as his or her replacement. Congratulations. You're there because you earned the position, but be careful not to move too quickly. If you're taking over the leadership of a team with a well-established system in place, it's not really a good idea to come in and make too many changes too quickly.

You probably have a lot of great ideas, and that's good, but you need to implement them slowly. If you come into it with all guns blazing and changing everything all at once, it will be a disruption rather than an improvement, so just relax. Enjoy the new position for a while before gutting the place. You're more than likely used to the old system yourself, and you're not going anywhere, so take your time. You can work with it.

And when you do start making changes, try spreading them out over time, a little here, a little there. Work them in gradually and slowly. It will make things much easier for everybody to adjust to. You also need to take into consideration that there are people who simply don't like change, but they also know change is inevitable, so they almost always do end up coming around. Just don't jam it down their throats. And then there are also some people who do like change, but even they will find it much easier to adjust with a more gradual introduction.

Where to Begin

Start by making a list of your ideas, followed by organizing it, prioritizing the changes you'd like to see happen first. Then, beginning with the first item on your list, make your first change and see how that goes. Get feedback from the other team members. And once it seems like everybody has adjusted well to that change, go on and move to the next item on your list. You might also find that this approach will take some pressure off you as well.

Feedback Is Important

Yes, it is, and for a few reasons:

- This is a team, and there's no "I" in team.
- It makes other team members feel important.
- It shows our flexibility, and we do need to be flexible.
- It makes us aware of what's working and what isn't.

You may not like all the feedback you hear, but you did agree to lead the team; therefore, you put yourself in the position where you have no choice but to listen. And if you don't agree with me about this, you need to remember that this is church and most, if not all, of the team is made up of volunteers, which we'll go into a little bit deeper in a later chapter.

Therefore, change your hearts and stop being stubborn.
—Deuteronomy 10:16 (NLT)

Yes. You are the team leader, but you're also a team member, so you must lead shoulder to shoulder and not from upon a pedestal. Jesus didn't even exalt Himself above His twelve chosen disciples. Both Matthew 20:28 (NLT) and Mark 10:45 (NLT) say, "For even the Son of Man came not to be served but to serve others and to give his life as a ransom for many." I don't think anyone is going to expect you to give up your life, but you must give up your pride.

New Rules

You probably have many great ideas for new rules or rule changes that you would like to implement. And there's nothing wrong with that, just as long as they don't go completely against the grain of the current rules and regulations. What I mean by that is, with a system already in place and working well, there's a certain level of comfort and familiarity within the team. And with any change, regardless of how minor it may seem to you, there can be negative reactions. I can't stress this strongly enough, but you must try to avoid any kind of negativity, even if it means that you will have to swallow your pride.

When pride comes, then comes shame;
But with the humble is wisdom.
—Proverbs 11:2 (NKJV)

Pride, as the Bible frequently points out, is a sin in God's eyes, so we really need to take Proverbs 11:2 to heart. It's easy to let pride rule us sometimes though. We may have an idea that sounds good to us and put it into action without even considering how it affects others. It may work for some too—but not for others. That's why we need to be careful about making changes to a system that works well, a system that everybody is comfortable with. Philippians 2:3 (NIV) says it best: "Do nothing out of selfish ambition or vain conceit. Rather, in humility value others above yourselves," So it really does come down to the old cliché, "If it ain't broken, don't fix it."

Be Flexible

Flexibility is extremely important when leading anything. It's great to have a vision, a plan, and desired goals. But as pointed out by Neil Anderson in a few of his books, "Who can block your goals? Everybody." Yes, that's right. *Everybody.* They usually don't do it on purpose—well, at least I hope not while serving God. We are all simply individuals, with different personalities, and we all have different ways of doing things. What might seem wrong to you may seem right to another and vice versa, so be flexible.

Blocked goals

When talking about blocked goals, Dr. Anderson points out that we set ourselves up for disappointments when we depend on others to meet our expectations, because they almost never do. We can often base our own success on how others meet our expectations, which also gives the enemy a foothold. Satan can feed off this to make us feel like failures, when in fact, we're really not failures. Think about it. How does somebody else's performance or lack thereof make us a failure? It doesn't. Why? Because we didn't do anything to fail, and the others may not have either. We simply don't all do things the same way as each other, and we need to learn to embrace that. By doing so, we have won a major battle against the kingdom of darkness, which is our primary goal to begin with.

We also need to take people's circumstances into consideration. For example, you were really depending on a member to be present, but he or she had car trouble and is late or can't make it to rehearsal. Now we all must have experienced that at some point, and we know that something like that is completely beyond anybody's control. Nobody did anything intentionally to you, but it still may have blocked your goal for that day.

That isn't to say that on occasion someone's intentional action won't block a goal or two, because sometimes it can happen. It's very unlikely that somebody will intentionally try to block your goal. It may just be a natural behavioral pattern for that person. So as a leader, it is your responsibility to figure out a way to work around it, especially when working with volunteers.

Why do you look at the speck that is in your brother's
eye, but do not notice the log that is in your own eye?
—*Matthew 7:3 (NASB)*

Off Limits

We don't always like the way other people do things, and it is in our nature to be critical, but we need to be very careful about what we're being critical of. We also shouldn't try to change a person's natural mannerisms. We can, however, ask people not to act in ways that may draw negative attention to themselves. We can also ask them not to do anything that could be considered offensive, not only to others, but primarily to God.

As members of any music ministry, we all need to focus on why we're doing it and not how. It's all about God. It's all about what Jesus did for us on the Cross and not about us. We may be performers in our other musical endeavors, and that's OK. But in church, we're playing for God. We're spiritual leaders. Above all, we represent God's Kingdom, so we all need to do it in such a way that it is pleasing in His eyes, not ours.

So what do I mean by off limits? The way a person naturally moves while playing or singing can sometimes look out of place in church. But if it's something you can live with and it doesn't bother or offend anybody, we might consider letting it slide. Pointing things like that out to people can make them self-conscious of it, and that can affect how they play or sing by causing them to focus on the visual aspect rather than the musical. We want our members to be proper representatives, but we also want them to be relaxed and comfortable while serving. God wants us all to be natural, the way He created us.

Old versus New

Please excuse me if it sounds like I'm going off on a little tangent here, but if you bear with me, hopefully, you'll understand why I included this section. I've had conversations with people who say that the Old Testament is obsolete, because it has been replaced by the New Testament. It sounds like it makes sense, but none of them can explain why, and the reason is because it's simply not true. My theory is that some people could be confusing two similar-sounding words, *covenant* and *testament*, for both of which there are new and old.

The Old Testament

There is nothing at all in the New Testament anywhere stating that the Old Testament is obsolete. In fact, it's quoted quite frequently in the New Testament, not only by the apostles, but also by Jesus Himself, and for a few very good reasons:

- It was the only Scripture they had to go by at the time.
- Jesus is and always will be the fulfillment of the Old Testament Scriptures.
- It is the unchanging Word of God.

There are some parts of the Old Testament, however, that may no longer apply—the old sacrificial system, for example, because Jesus is the Final and Perfect Sacrifice. The Old Covenant also no longer applies because it was replaced by the New Covenant, and that is possibly where the confusion comes in.

The New Covenant

In the Old Covenant, the high priest was the only person allowed to enter the Holy of Holies into the Presence of God, and he did so only once a year on the Day of Atonement for the atonement of our sins. And in the New Covenant, Jesus is the High Priest. When the veil that separated us from God was torn, we were granted permanent access to God's Presence any time of every day through what Jesus did for us on the Cross.

Like I said, this is only a theory on my part, but I believe that could be where some people are getting confused. So to simplify it, the New Covenant replaces the Old Covenant, but the New Testament does not replace the Old Testament. They are both valid and work together, because the old laws still apply.

The New Testament

Jesus came for a few main reasons:

- to give His life as a ransom for many
- to call sinners to repentance
- to give us eternal life
- to undo the work of Satan

He also came to do other things. Many of them continue to this day and are everlasting. Christianity, for example, resulted from what Jesus did for us on the Cross and in the grave. Without Him, it would never have existed. With the beginning of His human life also came the beginning of the New Testament. With His resurrection came the beginning of the Church. But we must not overlook what came along with His death on the Cross when the veil was torn: the New Covenant.

One of the earthly duties Jesus performed before ascending into Heaven was the merging of the Old Testament and New Covenant. Together, they make up the New Testament. So in effect, Jesus kept the best part of what was old and combined it with what's new, and He did this without completely gutting the place. We, even in our flesh, haven't been completely remodeled. Our physical bodies are the same bodies we were born with. It's our hearts, our minds, and our souls that changed when we were reborn.

Don't copy the behavior and customs of this world, but
let God transform you into a new person by changing
the way you think. Then you will learn to know God's
will for you, which is good and pleasing and perfect.
—Romans 12:2 (NLT)

So when you sign the papers on your new home, and before you go in tearing the place apart, bring in the couch and set up the TV. Sit back, relax, and invite some friends over to watch some football. Who knows? Maybe the old place will grow on you. There's really no urgency to create more work for yourself than you need to. Our physical life is too short for that anyway, so enjoy it.

Jesus Christ is the same yesterday and today and forever.
—Hebrews 13:8 (NIV)

Everyone thinks of changing the world, but
no one thinks of changing himself.
—Leo Tolstoy

CHAPTER 3

No Place for Bullies

When Haman saw that Mordecai neither bowed down
nor paid homage to him, Haman was filled with rage.
—Esther 3:5 (NASB)

Then Zeresh his wife and all his friends said to him,
"Have a gallows fifty cubits high made and in the
morning ask the king to have Mordecai hanged on it;
then go joyfully with the king to the banquet." And the
advice pleased Haman, so he had the gallows made.
—Esther 5:14 (NASB)

Then Harbonah, one of the eunuchs who were before the
king said, "Behold indeed, the gallows standing at Haman's
house fifty cubits high, which Haman made for Mordecai who
spoke good on behalf of the king!" And the king said, "Hang
him on it." So they hanged Haman on the gallows which he
had prepared for Mordecai, and the king's anger subsided.
—Esther 7:9–10 (NASB)

As I was preparing to begin the first grade, except for the horrors I witnessed from my parents' divorce, I was a happy-go-lucky little boy. I was looking forward to making new friends, which I did, but I also encountered something I had not considered: bullies. I can remember the first one too. I was scared. I didn't know what to do, so I started crying. And the more I cried, the more he bullied me. But much to my relief, two brothers came and chased him away. So every time after that, when the bully came, all I had to do was yell for them, and the two brothers would come running. I still keep in contact with two of them. In fact, just today, I was texting with one of the brothers, and the bully stops by to visit whenever he's in the area. It's funny how things change when we grow up.

I'm a fairly emotional person, so there would be times I would be sitting in class thinking about my parents, and I'd begin crying, for what seemed to be for no reason to everybody else. It made me an easy target for bullies. The other kids would start picking on me just to get me to cry more. And the more I cried, the more they bullied me. This continued for a few years, but it was somewhat manageable, because friends would defend me.

Then near the beginning of seventh grade, I was attending a high school football game, and out of nowhere came one of the bullies from the past. He grabbed me by the jacket to fling me to the ground like he always used to do, but this time, I stood solid. He tried again and failed and then again and failed. Then as we both realized that I was actually stronger than he was, the look of fear came over his face, and I began to smile. So he ran off and I chased after him. I caught him and flung him to the ground this time. Then he ran away and never bothered me again.

A few days later in school, another bully from the past knocked the books out of my hands in the hall, so I pushed him down and walked away feeling pretty good. I began seeking out the other bullies, but I didn't stop at that. I started picking fights for no reason and caused all sorts of trouble. That was when I started hiding behind a facade, and I became something I'm not: a bully.

My plan was working though. Because not only did I manage to make almost everybody afraid of me, but I also stopped the bullying. What I didn't realize was, that although I was keeping myself safe, I was also losing friends, and I wasn't very well liked, which wasn't part of my plan. I also began to realize how lonely it really was on that bench in front of the principal's office. It's probably a good thing that I sold that guillotine. Don't laugh. I'm not kidding.

All Shapes and Sizes

Bullying can take many forms, but the bullies all have a few things in common: the need to feel more important than others and to be in control of everything by using dominance and submission. So by bullying someone, we are trying to force the person into submitting to us, very much like what Haman was trying to do to Mordecai in the opening verses.

Nobody is 100 percent safe from all bullies, as we can see in the news every day. Murderers, thieves, rapists, and many other criminals are all bullies. They're not arrested for bullying, but that is, in reality, what they are doing. By making someone submit to them, they are bullying their victims in a major way. We see it in all walks of life and at all levels of authority. And as we have also seen in the news, churches aren't exempt from it either. We'll be looking at some of the ways that bullying can manifest itself along with some possible sources of it and also how God will help us at winning the battle so we can prevent it before it happens.

For wicked and deceitful mouths are opened against me,
speaking against me with lying tongues. They encircle me
with words of hate, and attack me without cause. In return
for my love they accuse me, but I give myself to prayer. So
they reward me evil for good, and hatred for my love.
—*Psalm 109:2–5 (ESV)*

The Enemy Within

We are all capable of being bullies, and sometimes we don't even realize that we're doing it. That's why, as I mentioned in the first chapter, it's helpful to be able to read people. The expression on a person's face will not only not only give us a pretty good clue as to how that person is feeling, but it's also a good indication of how we are treating him or her. As church leaders, we do need to be extremely aware of how we're treating others—not only for their benefit, but for everybody's—because as leaders, we should be setting good examples for our young up-and-coming leaders.

So if we are bullying and don't realize that we are, where is this behavior coming from? It could be any number of things, but some of the most common sources are the following:

- past trauma from being bullied or mistreated
- rejection or past failures
- learned behavior from bad examples
- lack of discipline or being spoiled
- demonic influence

These are just a few examples, but they can be used by the enemy as tools to influence us. And believe me, he will use them. He won't give up either. If one doesn't work, he'll move on to another or just wait for an opportunity to present itself.

And we all know, as I mentioned in chapter 1, he's clever, and he's also relentless. He will use us to beat down another person's self-confidence, and bullying is a perfect way for him to do just that. By doing so, he won't stop the growth of God's Kingdom, but he might slow it down, because those of us who lack confidence will be less likely to try drawing people closer to God.

Though a mighty army surrounds me, my heart will not be afraid. Even if I am attacked, I will remain confident.
—Psalm 27:3 (NLT)

Regardless of where our bullying nature comes from, we are fully responsible for our own actions. Satan and his adversaries cannot make us do anything. They can only put thoughts and suggestions into our minds and make us think they're our own. The three main weapons they commonly use against us are deception, temptation, and accusation, but they will also use our own weaknesses. Let's say, for example, if I had known sooner that I was capable of defending myself, I may never have become a bully at all. I would have had the confidence I needed to stand up to the other bullies, and I could have done it in a way that would've prevented me from losing my friends and getting myself into trouble. But instead, I gave the devil a foothold, and he used it against me.

The enemy allowed the hurt and anger I felt from being bullied to build up in me. Then along with that, he took the good feeling I got from defeating a couple of bullies and led me to believe that I was justified in being a bully and a troublemaker. I knew that my behavior was wrong, yet I chose to do it anyway. Then as I sat alone waiting for the principal, the accusation and reality of what I was doing began to set in. But then the next day, I'd be right back at it again. It took me a while to learn, but eventually, I did.

Soon after I got involved with music and playing in bands, I was beginning to make new friends, and I also regained some of my old ones. It took me until about halfway through the tenth grade, but I was finally enjoying school the way I had pictured it to be before I began first grade. Sure, I still got into fights. I kept getting myself into trouble too, but it was just the normal teenage stuff at that point.

Abuse of Authority

In the opening verses, we can see that Haman became angry with Mordecai for not bowing down to him. Then the advice from his wife and friends eventually led to him becoming a victim of his own anger. There are more details to the story, which you can find in the book of Esther, but to make it brief, Haman was elevated to a high position, second only to the king, and his authority went to his head. He expected everyone to bow down to him. So in effect, he became a bully.

This can happen to any of us, and I will admit to being guilty of it as well. I'm not writing this book to say I know the correct method to lead, so follow my example. I am only sharing mistakes that I have made, along with some I've observed others make. One of the biggest mistakes that we all make, and it happens in every facet of our lives, is to listen to the wrong voice. As I keep mentioning, and will continue to do so, God will never put negative thoughts or suggestions into our minds; He will also never give us the idea to exalt ourselves over others, so we need to catch ourselves when we begin doing it.

We will be benefiting everybody if we are more conscientious about our thoughts and if we carefully consider all possible consequences before acting on them. We must discern where the thought is coming from. And if we're still not sure, ask God for help. He wants to help us.

What then is my reward? That, when I preach the Good News, I may present the Good News of Christ without charge, so as not to abuse my authority in the Good News.
—1 Corinthians 9:18 (WEB)

Be Fruitful

Along with bringing every thought captive into obedience, which we will cover more in the next chapter, we must also be living by the fruit of the Spirit. Because, by doing so, we'll be treating others in a way that is the opposite of bullying.

But the fruit of the Spirit is love, joy, peace, patience, kindness, goodness, faithfulness, gentleness, self-control; against such things there is no law. And those who belong to Christ Jesus have crucified the flesh with its passions and desires. If we live by the Spirit, let us also keep in step with the Spirit. Let us not become conceited, provoking one another, envying one another.
—Galatians 5:22–26 (ESV)

Love

When asked what is the greatest of all the commandments, Jesus answered,

"YOU SHALL LOVE THE LORD YOUR GOD WITH ALL YOUR HEART, AND WITH ALL YOUR SOUL, AND WITH ALL YOUR MIND.' This is the great and foremost commandment. The second is like it, 'YOU SHALL

LOVE YOUR NEIGHBOR AS YOURSELF. On these two commandments depend the whole Law and the Prophets." (Matthew 22:37–40 NASB)

And when you think about what Jesus is saying here, it really makes all the sense in the world. Because if we all truly did love God and each other just as Jesus says we should, we would never sin against each other, there would be no need for any of the other commandments, and none of us would've ever been bullies in the first place.

Joy
The way we treat others can greatly affect how they feel, not only about themselves, but also about life in general. We can be mean and make them feel sad, angry, or sorrowful. Or we can be pleasant and give them great joy, which we can share in. As Proverbs 15:23 (NIV) states, "A person finds joy in giving an apt reply—and how good is a timely word!" Bullies don't do that.

Peace
In John 14:27 (NASB), Jesus says, "Peace I leave with you; My peace I give to you; not as the world gives do I give to you. Do not let your heart be troubled, nor let it be fearful." Jesus left us with His peace because He wanted us not only to have it for ourselves but also to share it with everyone. Peace comes through friendship and respect for each other. Peace comes through our love and fills us with joy. Bullies don't give peace, because they're not at peace.

Patience
All through the Bible, we read about patience. Most translations of First Corinthians 13:4 begin with "Love is patient, Love is

kind," and it truly is. Patience shows love, it gives joy, and it brings peace. We all learn, grow, and work at different paces, and we can get the best results from others if we allow them to go at their pace and not ours. If you're a fast-paced person, it's easy to become impatient. I know because I'm one. I had to learn to be patient, and I still need to work on it. So if God can be so patient with us, shouldn't we also be? To do otherwise is just another form of bullying.

Kindness
And in Ephesians 4:32 (NASB), Paul said, "Be kind to one another, tender-hearted, forgiving each other, just as God in Christ also has forgiven you." I think the word *kindness* speaks for itself. Acts of kindness certainly make people feel good. It makes us all feel loved and appreciated, things that bullies don't do or can't relate to.

Goodness
Very much like kindness, *goodness* also speaks for itself. We treat people kindly out of the goodness of our hearts. If we do good for others, they will do good for us in return. "Do not be overcome by evil, but overcome evil with good" (Romans 12:21 NIV). If I may give my own translation of this, I would say, "Do not allow a bully to control or intimidate you. But with a kind act of goodness, show grace and plant the seed of peace in the bully's heart."

Faithfulness
"Let not steadfast love and faithfulness forsake you; bind them around your neck; write them on the tablet of your heart" (Proverbs 3:3 ESV). Not only are we to remain faithful to God, but we must also be faithful to ourselves and each other. Being

faithful means we are true to our word, true to the facts, and true to others. We're honest and dependable. These are other traits you won't find in bullies, because they lack faith and are afraid to trust.

Gentleness

"A gentle answer turns away wrath, but a harsh word stirs up anger" (Proverbs 15:1 NIV). I think that pretty much says it all. And when you come right down to it, all the fruits of the Spirit are ways of expressing love, so they're all tied in together. There's probably no need for me to say this, but I will anyway. Bullies do not treat others with love, joy, peace, patience, kindness, goodness, faithfulness, or gentleness, which now brings us to our final and all-important fruit.

Self-Control

This fruit is not only self-explanatory, but it's also much more than just a biblical concept. Self-control is something we all need to be practicing, and I know this one all too well myself. There are many things that can and will cause us to lose control: sinful desires or temptations, anger or any number of other emotions. That's why we need to take all thoughts captive and do what's right in God's eyes—think before we act, sit back and take a deep breath, or just walk away and clear our heads. Bullies have no self-control; that's why they feel the need to control others.

For this very reason, make every effort to add to your faith goodness; and to goodness, knowledge; and to knowledge, self-control; and to self-control, perseverance; and to perseverance, godliness; and to godliness, mutual affection; and to mutual affection, love.
—2 Peter 1:5–7 (NIV)

Sticks and Stones

Sticks and stones will break my bones, and names will break my spirit. I'm rubber, and you're glue, and so are those words that are coming from you. Yes, that's right. Names do hurt, and words can also hurt and stick like glue. That's why we need to choose all our words wisely. Or as I like to put it, we must not allow our mouths to work faster than our brains. I remember watching an episode of *Wings* years ago, and Helen (Crystal Bernard) said a great line that always stuck with me. I'm not sure if this is verbatim, and I couldn't find it, but it went something like this: "Don't you wish sometimes that you could just suck those words right back into your mouth?"

The look on a person's face will tell us a lot about what we just said to him or her. Sometimes, though, as Helen pointed out, there are times we just know as soon as we hear ourselves saying it that it's something we should never have said. So it's extremely important, especially for us leaders, to be careful about what we say to people and also what we say about them. Words are extremely powerful. They can edify a person or just as easily demoralize somebody. As leaders, it's our responsibility to edify others.

> *Gracious words are a honeycomb, sweet to the soul and healing to the bones.*
> —*Proverbs 16:24 (NIV)*

Confrontation

There will be those times when we need to confront others for any number of reasons. But regardless of the reason, we always need to do it in a non-confrontational way, and we need to put others at ease. We must not make them feel like they're under attack or under the microscope. We must always be living by the fruit of the Spirit, and Jesus is our example to follow. So if we're treating others in a way that Jesus wouldn't, we certainly shouldn't be evaluating other people. We should be reevaluating ourselves. And if I may paraphrase Leo Tolstoy's quote from the previous chapter, "Everyone thinks about changing everybody else, but no one thinks of changing themselves."

> *And why do you look at the speck in your brother's eye, but do not perceive the plank in your own eye? Or how can you say to your brother, 'Brother, let me remove the speck that is in your eye,' when you yourself do not see the plank that is in your own eye? Hypocrite! First remove the plank from your own eye, and then you will see clearly to remove the speck that is in your brother's eye.*
> —*Luke 6:41–42 (NKJV)*

God's Protection

When I was in the ninth grade, I was only an in inch shorter than I am now, so I was fairly tall for my age. I played linebacker for our freshman football team and started every game. Seven years later, I played on a semi-pro team, I was a free safety, and I didn't start any games. Anybody who understands football knows there's quite a bit of size difference between those two positions, not only in height but also in weight and strength.

You might be asking, "What's your point?"

> *"I was born with nothing, and I will die with nothing. The LORD gave, and now he has taken away. May his name be praised!"*
> —*Job 1:21 (GNT)*

When I needed the strength to protect myself from bullies, God provided it. And when I abused that strength, He took it away.

You don't build up the weak ones, don't heal the sick, don't doctor the injured, don't go after the strays, don't look for the lost. You bully and badger them.
—*Ezekiel 34:4 (MSG)*

No being is so important that he can usurp the rights of another.
—Jean-Luc Picard

CHAPTER 4

———— ❧ ————

The Next Chapter

Don't be like the people of this world, but let God
change the way you think. Then you will know how
to do everything that is good and pleasing to him.
—Romans 12:2 (CEV)

As I'm getting further into writing this book, I am beginning
to realize how interrelated a lot of this subject matter is, and
I'm finding it more difficult to sort and separate it. As you may
have noticed in the first three chapters, I've referenced a later
chapter and the next chapter, which also triggered my sense
of humor for naming some of the chapters. This chapter, for
example, will focus on renewing our minds so that God can
help us think more like a shepherd than a king—in other words,
more like Jesus. I was originally going to name this chapter "To
Think or Not to Think."

All of these chapters do tie in together. So by the time
we get to the end of the book, they should all be working
together in our minds. Think of it this way: When we attend
a service at church or a Bible study group, when we pray or
read devotionals, when we read the Bible or a Christian book,

or when we have a private conversation with God, it all ties in together, and it also ties into this book. It's all part of our learning and growing together as we walk down that straight and narrow path with Jesus.

"Go in through the narrow gate, because the gate to hell is wide and the road that leads to it is easy, and there are many who travel it. But the gate to life is narrow and the way that leads to it is hard, and there are few people who find it.
—Matthew 7:13–14 (GNT)

I Didn't Think

Now I'm just as guilty of this as anybody else is, but how many times do we hear an excuse that begins with those three words? "I didn't think ..." And when we come right down to it, there's really no need to complete that sentence. Why? Because those three words say it all. Now imagine this: You're speeding down the road and get pulled over. The cop asks for your license and registration and asks if you know why you're being pulled over. And you say, "Yes, I was speeding."

Then he says, "That's right. You were doing eighty-four in a thirty-mile-per hour zone."

And just as you begin saying, "But, Officer, I didn't think ..." you pause because you draw a blank and can't think of anything else to say.

So he says, "You didn't think? Well, if I had known that, I wouldn't have stopped you. Here's your license and registration. Just slow down and be careful. There are a lot of careless drivers out there."

Please excuse my warped sense of humor, but how ridiculous is that story? About as ridiculous as those three words, right?

Well, first of all, every action is preceded by a thought of some sort. It may be an impulse, but that still involves a brief thought. It could be a suggestion or a well-thought-out plan, but there's always some preceding thought, so we need to be careful about our thoughts and even more careful about how we respond to them.

In her daily devotional *Battlefield of the Mind*, on Day 8, titled "As We Focus," Joyce Meyer says, "Where the mind goes, the man follows!" and how true that is. She explains that if we think about something long enough, we'll end up following through with that thought. I also personally like the title she uses for Day 36: "Think About What You Are Thinking About." For me, that really says it all. We need to do exactly that in order to take our thoughts captive. So think about it, no pun intended: we need to think about our thoughts and evaluate them so that we're able to discern where they're coming from before acting on them.

Trust in the LORD with all your heart; do not depend on your own understanding. Seek his will in all you do, and he will show you which path to take.
—Proverbs 3:5–6 (NLT)

Why Do You Ask?

I'm going to sidetrack a little here, because an interesting question just came up. Why am I putting a chapter about renewing our mind in a book about leading a church band? For me, and as I think it should be for any Christian, it is quite simple. When we first come to Christ, renewing our minds is something important that we need to learn about, because it plays a big part in us breaking our old worldly habits and developing new Christ-like habits. As a leader at any level in a church, we're setting examples, so we need to be setting good ones. And even if we fool the public, we cannot fool God, because He always knows what we're actually thinking.

> *"As for you, my son Solomon, know the God of your father, and serve Him with a loyal heart and with a willing mind; for the LORD searches all hearts and understands all the intent of the thoughts. If you seek Him, He will be found by you; but if you forsake Him, He will cast you off forever.*
> —*1 Chronicles 28:9 (NKJV)*

By the Book

I'm not sure where the cliché "by the book" actually came from, and I was unable to find it, so I'm just going to give the credit to an unknown author for that. The word *Bible* comes from the Greek word *biblion*, meaning "book." The Greek words *ta biblia* mean "the books." Now I'm sure that I'm not the first to come up with this, so I'm not taking credit here, but if you put "ta biblion" together, you get "the Book," or "the Bible." So when referring to *the Book*, I'm actually referring to the Bible. Now the Bible, from beginning to end, has many Scriptures about our minds and how we should think and conduct ourselves in a manner that is pleasing to God.

We're going to focus now on all the authors of the New Testament and their true-life examples of renewed hearts and minds.

> *For as he thinks within himself, so he is.*
> —*Proverbs 23:7 (NASB)*

Peter, Paul, and Mary—wait a minute. That's not right. Let me try again. John, Paul, George, and Ringo … No, that's not it either. Ah, I think I've got it now, so let me try one more time. Matthew, Mark, Luke, John, Paul, James, Peter, Jude, and, most importantly, Jesus are the authors of the New Testament, and here's what each one of them has set before us to follow.

Matthew

Unlike Mark and Luke, who both call him by his old name Levi, he refers to himself as Matthew the tax collector. Matthew is his new name, which was given to him by Jesus. It means "Gift of the Lord," but Matthew is more than likely reminding us, as well as himself, of his past in order to set a good example and show that we have the ability to change the way we think, live, and act and how we treat others. He was in his tax collector's booth just doing his job at the time, when Jesus walked by and said to him, "Follow Me." Matthew then stepped out of his booth and left it all behind to follow Jesus (Matthew 9:9, Mark 2:14, and Luke 5:27–28). Tax collectors were not very well liked in those days, not that we like them any better today, but he had a change of heart and mind and began to follow the right path with Jesus, as is made evident by his authorship of the first book of the New Testament, The Gospel According to Matthew.

Mark

Also known as John Mark, he wasn't one of the twelve disciples, but he was believed to be the young man who followed Jesus before and after His arrest, which may be why it's also believed that he wrote the second gospel and second book of the New Testament, Mark, based on his own eyewitness accounts. Mark also went along with Paul and Barnabas on a mission trip to Antioch, but he bailed out on them early, so Paul had lost his trust in him for a time and didn't want him to go with them on the next journey. Barnabas did want Mark to go, however, so Barnabas and Paul went their separate ways. And with that second chance that Barnabas had given him, Mark proved himself to be worthy. As Paul later indicated in one of his letters to Timothy, he regained his confidence in Mark and called for him from prison: "Only Luke is with me. Pick up Mark and bring him with you, for he is useful to me for service." (2 Timothy 4:11 NASB). So we can see that at some point Mark had a change of heart and mind and later was also an assistant to Peter in the early Church.

Luke

The only non-Jewish author of the New Testament. Although he wasn't one of Jesus' disciples, nor did he bear witness to Jesus' ministry, he left no stone unturned during his research, as we can see in his investigative writing of the third gospel, also the third book of the New Testament, Luke. Luke the physician, as he was known by his profession, also authored the book of Acts, where he focuses mainly on the acts of Peter and Paul, and the coming of the Holy Spirit. This is extremely significant because the Holy Spirit is who guides us and empowers us today just as He did with the early members of the Church on the Day of Pentecost. The conviction of our sin and the renewing of our minds and hearts also depend very much on the Holy Spirit. And as Jesus said to His disciples before He ascended into Heaven, "but you will receive power when the Holy Spirit has come upon you; and you shall be My witnesses both in Jerusalem, and in all Judea and Samaria, and even to the remotest part of the earth." (Acts 1:8 NASB).

John

One of the first disciples and author of the fourth and final gospel, which is also the fourth book of the New Testament,

"John". He refers to himself as "the disciple Jesus loved." He walked away from his profession as a fisherman when Jesus called to him. John, along with Peter and James, made up Jesus' inner circle. They followed Jesus closely and were included in private prayers and events, which none of the other disciples were, such as the transfiguration. John was also the author of three epistles and the book of Revelation, in which he instructs us to love and obey the commandments of Christ, to live in fellowship with the Lord, and to live as children of God. He also gives us clear warnings of false prophets and false teachers and advises us to beware of deceivers. In finale, he shares his visions in order to prepare us for the final and triumphant return of Jesus. One of my favorite quotes from him is "Do not love the world nor the things in the world. If anyone loves the world, the love of the Father is not in him" (1 John 2:15 NASB).

Paul

Originally known as Saul of Tarsus and author of nearly half of the New Testament, Paul has had perhaps the most dramatic life-, mind-, and heart-changing experience of all. Many early Christians had faced persecution, imprisonment, and death by Saul's hand. But while on his way to Damascus, Saul had an encounter with Jesus.

> As he neared Damascus on his journey, suddenly a light from heaven flashed around him. He fell to the ground and heard a voice say to him, "Saul, Saul, why do you persecute me?" "Who are you, Lord?" Saul asked. "I am Jesus, whom you are persecuting," he replied. "Now get up and go into the city, and you will be told what you must do." (Acts 9:3–6 NIV).

You can read the rest of the story in Acts, but after that, he was transformed from Saul the persecutor to Paul the apostle and became an extremely important leader of the early church. That's what I call renewing of the mind.

James

Not to be confused with the disciple of the same name, this James is a brother of Jesus and author of the New Testament book titled James. He didn't follow Jesus during His ministry. In fact, he did quite the opposite. Jesus wasn't exactly popular in His hometown. And during one of Jesus' visits, James, along with his siblings and other locals, were threatening to throw Jesus off a cliff. So I guess like "Doubting Thomas," James needed to see in order to believe. And judging by the book of James, he most certainly did believe and became a great church leader.

> *What use is it, my brethren, if someone says he has faith but he has no works? Can that faith save him?*
> *—James 2:14 (NASB)*

Peter

Simon Peter became one of Jesus' closest disciples shortly after leaving his career as a fisherman behind. That, of course, was a major change for him, but that wasn't the end of his makeover. He was known for having impulsive and sometimes violent outbursts, such as when he cut off the ear of a servant who was assisting in the arrest of Jesus. He had also denied Jesus three times, for which he expressed great remorse. And through all his own acts of being temperamental and somewhat rebellious, he proved to be his own best example of how not to behave. He had a change of heart and mind and became a leader of the early church. He wrote two of the epistles in the New Testament and was a true living example for all of us to follow.

For we did not follow cleverly devised tales when we made known to you the power and the coming of our Lord Jesus Christ, but we were eyewitnesses of His majesty.
—*2 Peter 1:16 (NASB)*

Jude

One of the shortest books in the Bible, Jude was written by another brother of Jesus of the same name, Jude. He, like their brother James, was not an original follower of Jesus during His ministry. Jude also needed more proof, and it took a crucifixion and resurrection to convince him. Along with James, he was a leader of the Jerusalem church for Jewish Christians living in the Mediterranean. In his epistle to them, he gave warnings of false teachers and prophets. Jude also had a change of heart and mind. In fact, I think John, Paul, George and Ringo also wrote a song about him. Just kidding, but I'll bet I had some of you wondering.

I say this because some ungodly people have wormed their way into your churches, saying that God's marvelous grace allows us to live immoral lives. The condemnation of such people was recorded long ago, for they have denied our only Master and Lord, Jesus Christ.
—*Jude 1:4 (NLT)*

Why These Men?

The Bible is filled with many great examples of righteous people who underwent changes of heart, mind, soul, and attitude to follow God and Jesus. And I could have chosen any one or any group of them. In fact, I could have chosen all of them, but that would've taken up an entire book in itself. And that book has already been written. It's called the Holy Bible.

The reason I chose these men is because of what they all have in common. They all gave up everything to follow Jesus and lead us all into Christianity. They took the torch as Jesus handed it to them and kept marching forward with it. And upon the foundation Jesus laid for them, they built the Church, which is still standing today.

They all authored books in the New Testament and set examples for all of us to follow. But as important as what they all did for us is, we mustn't overlook the most important Author and Example of the New Testament, the most important Leader and True Founder of the Church, the True Shepherd to us all.

Jesus

Although He never actually penned a book in the Bible, He's still the most important Author. He's the author of life. And although he didn't have a change of heart or mind, He's still our greatest example. Jesus is our King, our Shepherd, our Savior, and our Servant. He came to serve man and lead us to safety. He came to teach us how to live, how to lead, and how to follow. He came to give us His love so that we'll love one another. He came to give us His peace so that we'll share it with each other. He came to give us His mind so that we can renew ours and think like Him. He came to show us the way Home.

And though He is a King, He came and lived as a man, shoulder to shoulder with man. He came humbly in triumph and will return one day boldly in triumph. We should all learn from and follow His example.

FOR WHO HAS KNOWN THE MIND
OF THE LORD, THAT HE WILL INSTRUCT
HIM? But we have the mind of Christ.
—*1 Corinthians 2:16 (NASB)*

To Think or Not to Think

That is the question. You didn't think that I was going to conclude this chapter without sneaking that in, did you? And in case you are still wondering what the point of this chapter is, it's about having the right mind to lead. To lead like a shepherd, not a king, which is really the whole point of this book as well. But the importance of this chapter doesn't only apply to leaders. It applies to everybody. Yes, *everybody*. Whether you're a believer, a nonbeliever, or still on the fence, it's important to have a right mind to live right.

And though it sounds easier said than done, it begins with change, just as all the previously mentioned authors of the New Testament experienced, so let us learn from their examples.

We need to have the wisdom to carefully consider each and every thought before acting on it. We need to be able to consider all the possible consequences of our actions so that we can make right choices to take the right action in all situations. We need to renew our minds and take all thoughts captive, as the Bible says. And the more we practice, the better we'll get at it.

But one of the most important points Jesus is trying to teach us is to regard others as being more important than ourselves. That will more than likely be the biggest change we all need to make.

Brothers and sisters, think of what you were when you were called. Not many of you were wise by human standards; not many were influential; not many were of noble birth.
—*1 Corinthians 1:26 (NIV)*

If your speech is characterized by lots of "I," "me," and "my," you're focusing on yourself far too much.
—Charles F. Stanley

CHAPTER 5

Poking the Bees' Nest

They swarmed around me like bees, but they
were consumed as quickly as burning thorns; in
the name of the LORD I cut them down.
—Psalm 118:12 (NIV)

Bees will pretty much mind their own business and leave us alone unless they're provoked or feel threatened. I can remember when we were kids. My cousin and I were walking in his front yard and saw a bee hovering around a piece of gum on the walkway, so we killed it. Then a few minutes later, we walked by the same spot, and there was another bee there doing the same thing. So we killed that one too. My uncle was watching. He told us that bees have radar and send out distress signals when they're attacked or killed so that other bees will come to help and that if we keep doing it, a swarm will come and attack us. So what do you think we did? We stayed and kept doing it. So one by one, they kept on coming. And one by one, we kept right on killing them, but no swarm ever came, so we got bored and went in to race slot cars.

A few days later, we saw a very large hornet's nest up in a tree, so we tried to find a long enough stick to poke at it with. We couldn't find one, so we threw rocks instead. After a few minutes of finding out just how bad our aim was, one of us hit it and really good too. I don't know whose rock it was that hit, but it was dead center and tore the nest almost completely in half, so that the bottom part was just barely dangling there.

Lucky for us we were far enough away so we were able to run off before they could notice us. We crept back slowly to check it out, and boy were they angry. I mean really angry. There was a huge and frantic swarm. The sound was so frightening that we ran off again and didn't go back there until the next day. And believe it or not, they had completely repaired the nest so you couldn't tell that it had been damaged at all. But we did notice something different about it. It was considerably larger than it originally was. They left the bottom part hanging and added material to fill in the opening to join both sections together. We figured they were building a bigger nest for a bigger army. So needless to say, we didn't go back there again—well, not to that nest anyway. We just went back in to race slot cars again, which reminds me. I still have my slot cars. I should clear out a spot in the basement to set up the track.

The Sequel

This chapter is somewhat of a sequel to chapter 3, "No Place for Bullies." But before we got further into it, I wanted to break away from the subject so I could show you how important I think it is to have a change of heart and mind, not only to help us be better leaders, but also to help us get bullying under control. Here we will look at bullying from another perspective.

We're all capable of being bullies. And all of us have more than likely bullied someone at least once during our lives. Many of us could have done so unintentionally or without even knowing that we did it. However, many of us will do it quite intentionally. And in some cases, there could be a motive behind it, such as obtaining a desired goal or obstructing another person from achieving his or hers. In other cases, we simply need to feel like we are the ones who are in control of everyone, *and* everything.

> *Be strong and courageous. Do not be afraid or terrified because of them, for the* Lord *your God goes with you; he will never leave you nor forsake you."*
> *—Deuteronomy 31:6 (NIV)*

Common Denominator

One thing all bullies have in common is a victim. Sometimes the victims are chosen randomly, and sometimes they are intentional targets. But however a bully chooses his or her victims, it doesn't make it any less of a crime. Yes. Bullying is a crime any way you look at it. Why? Because it involves a victim. In fact, one of the definitions for crime in the *Merriam-Webster Dictionary* app puts it like this: "a grave offence especially against morality." Now can I make it any clearer than that? And if you don't agree, then go and ask somebody who has been bullied and see what they have to say about it. Or perhaps you yourself have been bullied. If so, how did it make you feel? Ah, so now you do agree.

Intentional Target

When a bully intentionally goes after a certain person, there's more than likely a motive behind it. It could be revenge, or he or she may just want something from the victim. The bully could also feel threatened or intimidated by the person because of an inferiority complex. One of the most common reasons for bullying, however, is quite often low self-esteem and the need to make him- or herself feel more important than everybody else. Another fairly common reason, as it can be with many personality traits, could be a learned behavior, perhaps from growing up in an abusive environment.

Random Target

Sometimes a bully will just go looking for somebody to pick on for no reason other than to appease his or her own ego. In this case, the victims are usually randomly chosen, but not always. These are the type of bullies that everybody keeps an eye on because nobody knows who, when, or where they're going to strike next. And their presence alone makes those around them feel uncomfortable, also causing a lot of tension. The bully enjoys this too because it makes him or her feel in control of everyone and everything, which is exactly what the bully wants: to be in control.

Spontaneous Target

There may be occasions when a person, and not necessarily one who is known to be a bully, will begin picking on another person for what may seem to be no apparent reason. This doesn't make it any less of an offense however. It really is cut and dry. Any way you look at it, bullying is bullying. It's wrong. It's offensive. And most of all, it's hurtful. We, as human beings, Christian or not, and especially leaders, must be protective of each other. And one of the best ways of doing this is not to be bullies in the first place.

Elisha left Jericho and went up to Bethel. As he was walking along the road, a group of boys from the town began mocking and making fun of him. "Go away, baldy!" they chanted.
"Go away, baldy!" Elisha turned around and looked at them, and he cursed them in the name of the LORD. Then two bears came out of the woods and mauled forty-two of them.
—2 Kings 2:23–24 (NLT)

No Place to Hide

The worst kind of bullies are the ones who feel the need to be constantly attacking someone. They will move from one victim to another, and their targets can be intentional, random, or spontaneous without any regard for who they are or why they have chosen them as victims. And while all bullies can be dangerous, these bullies tend to be the most violent type. They feel they have something to prove and will stop at nothing to prove it. But what are they actually proving? Nothing. That's right, absolutely nothing. Trust me. Because that's what I used to do, and all it gained me was a lot of trouble and fewer friends.

Be sober, be vigilant; because your adversary the devil, as a roaring lion, walketh about, seeking whom he may devour:
—1 Peter 5:8 (KJV)

Let's say you have a situation at your workplace where someone is being bullied. The bully is instructed to stay away from that person or face termination, and he or she does comply. The only problem is that bully will almost immediately find somebody else to go after, and if he or she can't bully anybody at work, that person will find a victim elsewhere. Now most bullies prefer not to bring their behavior into their homes. In fact, in many cases, their families are unaware of their bullying because of this. However, if all other avenues are blocked to finding victims, they'll resort to bullying members of their own family. This is usually a last resort though. But if it does occur, this is where they have the potential to become the most violent for any number of reasons, but here are just a few:

- They become angry because they feel forced to inflict harm on their family, who they're expected to protect, so out of frustration, they take it out on them.
- They sometimes begin to feel more comfortable bullying them because they feel, well, right at home.
- They can also find themselves blaming their family, which is somewhat of a contradiction, but they will rationalize it so they themselves don't have to take the blame.

Whatever the reason is, there is absolutely no plausible excuse for bullying, and it shouldn't be tolerated anywhere. Period. No matter what. Not in the workplace, not on the street, not in school, not at home, and not at church. Nowhere. So if you or somebody that you know is a bully or is being bullied, you need to take action.

If you're the target of a bully, you need to get help and protection immediately. If you're the one doing the bullying, you absolutely must do whatever is necessary to seek help to break this trend. God will get you through it, but you need to seek His face and let your pastor know you need help. Nobody is going to knock you for coming forward on your own because our Christian family is full of people who want to and will do anything they can to help you. God will work through them to help you.

The LORD said to Satan, "From where do you come?"
Then Satan answered the LORD and said, "From
roaming about on the earth and walking around on it."
—*Job 1:7 (NASB)*

Stop Poking

It's never a good idea to single out a person and constantly put him or her under attack. You may not like the way that person does things, but that doesn't mean he or she is doing it wrong, and it certainly doesn't justify a barrage of suggestions for improvement. So if you find yourself constantly disagreeing with someone and asking a person to change the way he or she does things, then you may want to consider the possibility that it could be you who needs to change. As Michael Jackson said in his hit song "Man in the Mirror," "Take a look at yourself, and then make a change."

Repeatedly poking a person, which is my polite way of putting it, can also bring out the worst in anybody. It can beat down a person's level of confidence and make him or her self-conscious and unable to perform to his or her full potential. It could also elicit an angry response, which is never a good thing. In many cases, we as Christians try to live up to a self-imposed standard, so we tend to bite our tongues in order to give a proper image of ourselves. The problem with that is, it can build internal anger, like a snowball. And if this happens, it can all come out in one big explosion.

Know Who You're Poking

It's also very important to know your team members, as we talked about in chapter 1. Yes, we are Christians, yet we are also humans; therefore, we have the potential to get defensive if we are insulted, and we all have different responses when defending ourselves.

Now we all know, or hopefully know, what can happen when we poke at a bees' nest. The bees become angry and defensive, and they attack in swarms. The more we poke, the angrier they get. We aren't much different. The more we get poked, the angrier we get, and we can also be provoked to attack.

Now suppose you're poking and keep poking and poking at what appears to be a small bees' nest. Then you poke just a little too hard and poke all the way through to the back side of it, only to find out it's attached to a much larger bees' nest. Do you see my point? Well, if not, then let me explain.

Anger can be contagious, just like many other emotions. And if you're making somebody angry because of the way you're treating a certain person, there's also the possibility that others can become angry and come to that person's defense. Then not only is it possible to create a schism within the church, but you can also hurt your own credibility as a leader by setting a bad example. And as I keep stressing—and I will continue to do so—we as team leaders truly need to be setting good examples, even if it means going against our own grains.

I will admit that I don't always like doing that; however, it almost always turns out for the best. Therefore, it really is a good idea to take off our blinders and stop looking through tunnel vision. You would be absolutely amazed at how much more successful it can make you feel. That, my friends, is why living by the fruit of the Holy Spirit is so important.

In the same way the Spirit also helps our weakness; for
we do not know how to pray as we should, but the Spirit
Himself intercedes for us with groanings too deep for
words; and He who searches the hearts knows what the
mind of the Spirit is, because He intercedes for the saints
according to the will of God. And we know That God causes
all things to work together for good to those who love
God, to those who are called according to His purpose.
—Romans 8:26–28 (NASB)

To the Bully

Please don't take any of this as a personal attack, because we
are all potentially nice people deep down inside. And yes,
even you are. Why? Because God made you that way. You
may fear being vulnerable or weak if you drop your facade.
But in reality, it will make you stronger and much, much
more respected. It will make you into a true leader, a true
living example for others to follow. You will lead like a true
shepherd.

Now we who are strong ought to bear the weaknesses of
those without strength and not just please ourselves.
—Romans 15:1 (NASB)

So please trust me when I tell you this, you will feel much
better about yourself for treating people with kindness than
you do when you bully them. Now wasn't that your original
intention? To feel better about yourself? And lo and behold, you
can accomplish it by simply being an outwardly nice person.
Imagine that.

To the Victim

It's not at all easy to be on the receiving end of a bully's attack, but please don't allow fear to prevent you from seeking help. There are many victims who will hide what they're going through because of fear. Some not only fear repercussions from the bully, but they may also fear rejection from their friends and family. Why? Because of low self-esteem, which will result from being bullied. The victim can also begin to believe he or she is worthless from demeaning things the bully has said. And believe it or not, sometimes victims will keep quiet just to protect the bullies.

> *Put on the full armor of God, so that you can*
> *take your stand against the devil's schemes.*
> *—Ephesians 6:11 (NIV)*

Now I'm not suggesting that you stand there and fight or argue with the bully. Just be aware of his or her evil schemes and how very much they are like Satan's. That's because they are, so seek help. "First seek the counsel of the LORD" (1 Kings 22:5 NIV). Also, pray for protection, and then ask to speak to a pastor. The bottom line is the bullying needs to stop, so do whatever it takes to achieve that, as long as it's within means that are acceptable to God.

To Our Pastors

It can be extremely difficult to accept the possibility that one of your team leaders is a bully. And when somebody comes to you for protection from such a person, it's easy to put on your blinders and take sides with the leader. You may have aided with elevating that person to a leadership position, and thus you could be more apt to try to reconcile the relationship between the leader and the member presenting the complaint so that you can keep the peace within the church without drawing attention to the situation.

Your biggest concern, however, should be the safety and the peace of mind of the person making a complaint. Being a leader absolutely doesn't make us automatically right, and you truly need to accept that. Some of the steps you can take in such a case are as follows:

- Be objective and willing to accept the possibility that there may be a legitimate complaint against the leader.
- Consider how often the person complains. If this is the first or only time, then the leader is possibly the problem.
- The number of incidents can be a clear indication that the leader could be the problem. Because if there are multiple incidents on one complaint, the person complaining may have been holding back in an effort to keep the peace.
- The complainer's response in each incident can also tell you a lot. If he or she has taken the high road most of or all the time, that's exhibiting self-control.
- The elapsed time between the first and most recent incident can indicate if the one complaining is a chronic complainer or not. It can also show how patient the person is.

These are only a few of the things to be considered but perhaps the most important ones. It's your job as a pastor to take all complaints very seriously until all the facts are in. Because if you choose to take sides with the leader and later find out that he or she was being dishonest, it's going to be quite a bit more difficult to reconcile the relationship—and not only between the person complaining and the leader but also between you and both of them.

> *My brothers and sisters, believers in our glorious Lord Jesus Christ must not show favoritism. Suppose a man comes into your meeting wearing a gold ring and fine clothes, and a poor man in filthy old clothes also comes in. If you show special attention to the man wearing fine clothes and say, "Here's a good seat for you," but say to the poor man, "You stand there" or "Sit on the floor by my feet," have you not discriminated among yourselves and become judges with evil thoughts?*
> *—James 2:1–4 (NIV)*

To Everybody

Hebrews 13:17 (NASB) says, "Obey your leaders and submit to *them*." I wanted to point this out because it is important that we recognize the authority of our team leaders and do submit to them. In Luke 14:3 (NASB), Jesus said, "Is it lawful to heal on the Sabbath, or not?" Now you may think that I'm comparing apples and oranges, but Jesus was constantly challenging authority. And He wasn't doing it to be rebellious or to teach us not to submit but to teach us about legalism versus discretion. There might be times when someone in leadership abuses his or her authority. And whether or not he or she intended to, we must have the freedom to use discretion, especially in a case where bullying is involved or the leader is being dishonest. In either case, we should not submit. We should seek help.

I'm not saying refuse to submit, unless of course the demand can be considered improper. But what I am suggesting is to first try to politely reason with the leader to see if the two of you can come to some kind of compromise. If the leader then refuses to listen or becomes unreasonable, do your best to comply until you're able to get assistance from somebody who can help. In other words, try to give the leader the benefit of the doubt before you bring it to a higher authority, because we already do have the highest authority working for us. God.

What then shall we say to these things? If
God is for us, who can be against us?
—Romans 8:31 (NKJV)

As Christians, we're part of one family—God's family. And He wants us to love and protect our family members, instead of judging them.
—Joyce Meyer

CHAPTER 6

Boundaries

You set all the boundaries of the earth, and
you made both summer and winter.
—Psalm 74:17 (NLT)

While I was in Australia, I noticed that every residential property had a fence around it, and most, if not all, of them were tall enough so you couldn't see over. Some of them were like structures that you could put a roof on and build a house around the house. And from what I understand, it's like that in many European countries as well. The people there are very much into security and feeling safe. And who wouldn't feel safe with a fortress around their yard? One thing was for certain though, there was absolutely no question in my mind as to where the property boundaries were.

Now back here in Massachusetts, as well as many other parts of the United States, it's much different. There are some properties with large fences, but there's also a much larger variety and many different sizes and styles of fences. You can see stockades, chain links, pickets, post-and-rails, barbed wire, and probably more that I can't think of right now. Some are for security, some are for pets or children, and some are just simply for decoration.

Then you'll see some properties divided by stone walls or rows of trees and shrubs. And quite often, you will also see a couple or even several homes in a row with nothing but open lawns between them. But even with those open lawns, there are still boundaries. We may not see them, but they are there. And trust me, the owners do know exactly where they are too. Many of our dogs also know where the boundaries are.

And very much like the properties with open lawns, people also have invisible boundaries, which we truly need to be very aware of, especially as leaders. In this chapter, we're going to talk about some of those boundaries, why it's extremely important that we avoid encroaching on them, and how to recognize when we have.

Varieties

Much like anything else, there are different types of boundaries for people. Some are written out, such as laws or rules and regulations. Some are implied, such as etiquette or moral standards. And some are invisible and unique to individuals, such as curfews or personal likes and dislikes. But whichever of these boundaries apply to any given situation, they must be respected and obeyed. We must also bear in mind that being a leader in no way gives us any exemption from this. In fact, it makes us even more responsible for respecting and obeying all such boundaries because it plays a fairly major role in the examples that we're setting for others.

> *Do not move an ancient boundary*
> *stone set up by your ancestors.*
> *—Proverbs 22:28 (NIV)*

Laws

Violations of legal boundaries can be tricky because they may vary from state to state or country to country, so we can't really be very specific here. Laws may also apply differently to paid employees than they do to volunteer help, so you might not be able to impose the same demands on both, which we will cover in more detail in a later chapter. But whichever the case may be, it would be very helpful to be somewhat familiar with the laws in your area and how they pertain to your situation. Or at the very least, have quick resources available in case you find yourself in need of legal advice.

There are many laws that we all automatically know apply everywhere, such as laws regarding sexual harassment or any type of physical assault. For example, I'm pretty sure that we all know that you can get yourself into a lot of trouble if you kill somebody, regardless of what your excuse may be. OK. There I go trying to be funny again, but I think you get the picture.

> *You shall thus observe My statutes and keep*
> *My judgements, so as to carry them out, that*
> *you may live securely on the land.*
> *—Leviticus 25:18 (NASB)*

Rules and Regulations

These are fundamentally like laws and generally governed by our laws, but they can vary based on the needs or requirements of the organization they pertain to. For example, one church may allow men to wear hats where another may not, even though the Bible is unquestionably clear about this point. We don't want to get off the subject here, so we'll cover that in chapter 11, "How and Why."

The Bible, however, does bring up a valid point that does

apply here. This could pertain more to laws than to rules and regulations. But the Bible is God's Word. It's the Law. And it is final. There isn't much I can add to that except read the Bible and follow it. Because by following the Bible, we can't go wrong.

We must first remember that we're serving God in His house, so we must follow His rules. And all through the Bible we will find rules and regulations pertaining to how to treat each other and how to show respect for each other. Being a leader in no way gives us the right to treat anybody with disrespect.

Implied Boundaries
These can be based on written laws, rules, and regulations but are also ways that we automatically know how we should and should not conduct ourselves in given situations or settings. For example, a man should show much more or different respect for a female friend than he would for a male friend and vice versa. But we still must show our respect for everybody regardless of gender.

Etiquette
A good example here could be a person shouldn't stand up during the flow of a church service and shout in a very loud voice, "Does anybody know what time the Patriots game starts tonight?" Ah, you can double-check me on this one, but I'm pretty sure that would be encroaching on everybody's boundaries, especially in the church I go to, because our pastor includes that information in his message. Just kidding, of course.

All joking aside, we should always treat people with respect when we as leaders are confronting them or if they're coming to us with a question or concern. We need to take them seriously and not try to downplay their concerns because there will be times when we consider some of their questions ridiculous or unimportant. But to the person who is addressing them, they could be very personal or embarrassing. So we need to listen carefully to make sure that we completely understand them and not give them any old answer just to pretend we're concerned. The point here is that any type of disrespect can be considered improper etiquette.

Moral Standards

Sometimes when people take moral standards too far, it can become legalism. We don't need to be walking on eggshells and worrying about every word we speak or action we take as long as it's in agreement with God's Word. The simplest way I can think of putting it is to live by the fruit of the Spirit, which I point out fairly frequently.

> *Let your gentleness be evident to all. The Lord is near.*
> *—Philippians 4:5 (NIV)*

I know I'm being very general on a lot of this, but I believe we also know all this. I'm simply trying to remind us all of things we don't constantly think about so we don't slip back into our worldly patterns and get ourselves into trouble.

Invisible Boundaries

What I'm talking about here is also tricky because it's personal and is unique for each individual. This is where reading people would be extremely helpful. As I mentioned in chapters 1 and 3, and probably will again, the look on a person's face can tell us quite a bit about what we said or how we may have acted toward him or her, so watch for red flags.

This is also where knowing a person's story can be extremely helpful. Let's say, for example, you have a team member who wakes up at 4:00 a.m. for work every day, and you ask him or her if you can speak for a few minutes after rehearsal, which ends at 8:30 p.m., and then you keep the person there until a little past 9:30 p.m. Then the next thing you know, "Old Jed's a millionaire." Wait a minute. I think I used that one already. Sorry. Anyway, the next thing you know, a pastor is asking to meet with you because that person has filed a complaint against you.

Now if you knew that team member gets up that early and usually goes to bed around 8:00 or 8:30 p.m., you would have known that he or she was already up past bedtime and needed to get home. And it's very unlikely that you would have kept that person there that late in the first place. So my suggestion is to first ask a person how late he or she can stay.

And if you think you'll need more time than that, try to agree on a time that's convenient for both of you to get together. Or if you say that it's only going to be for a few minutes, make sure it is only a few minutes. Being a team leader in no way whatsoever gives us license to impose any kind of inconvenience on anybody for any reason. If you don't agree, well then, you should absolutely not be in any type of leadership role. Period.

The LORD will tear down the house of the proud,
But He will establish the boundary of the widow.
—Proverbs 15:25 (NASB)

Privacy

We all love our own privacy, and we also expect everybody—and I do mean everybody—to respect it. Being a team leader absolutely does not give us the right to tell team members what they can and cannot do in the privacy of their own homes on their own time. First of all, and we'll cover this a bit more in a later chapter, most, if not all, of the members we're leading are volunteers. Therefore, what they do or don't do outside the church is absolutely off limits and none of our business, unless, of course, it's drawing negative attention to the church or God's Kingdom.

For example, if you ask somebody to work on certain aspects of their singing or playing a musical instrument and that person plays and practices on more than one instrument, you cannot impose which instruments he or she can and can't practice at home. And once again, if you don't agree, I think you know what I'm going to say here, so just learn to live with the fact that we need to respect the other members' privacy. Period.

It was very early in the morning and still dark.
Jesus got up and left the house. He went to a place
where he could be alone. There he prayed.
—*Mark 1:35 (NIRV)*

Financial Boundaries

I bring this up for good reason because I've seen this happen. If any team members are uncomfortable using certain equipment that has been provided by the church, then they should be allowed to bring in their own as long as it doesn't disrupt anything.

A good example I can give here is a bass drum pedal. Suppose a drummer has a problem with the feel of the church's pedal, so that drummer brings his or her own and uses an identical beater so it sounds exactly the same. There should be no problem allowing that person to do so. Or if somebody brings in a double bass pedal in order to play certain songs more accurately, then again, there should be no problem.

If we don't like him or her doing so, we should allow that person to make minor adjustments on the provided equipment. However, we should never ask anybody to spend his or her own money on equipment that is identical to the equipment provided by the church to practice with it at home. For one thing, that person more than likely isn't being paid to do this. And for another, we don't know what impact that will make on someone's financial situation. The bottom line here is that it's just not right to expect someone to invest his or her own money into musical equipment that he or she would have no other practical use for. It's a different story, however, if that person does so on his or her own, but we have no right to impose it on anybody.

> *may he equip you with all you need for doing his will. May he produce in you, through the power of Jesus Christ, every good thing that is pleasing to him. All glory to him forever and ever! Amen.*
> —*Hebrews 13:21 (NLT)*

Respect

As much as we want to be in control, because we are the leaders, we must treat everybody with respect. And when I say everybody, that's exactly what I mean. This doesn't apply only to how we relate with the team members; it includes how we interact with every single person we encounter—every place we go. Disrespect can also be considered a form of bullying.

But the Holy Spirit produces this kind of fruit in
our lives: love, joy, peace, patience, kindness,
goodness, faithfulness, gentleness, and self-
control. There is no law against these things!
—Galatians 5:22–23 (NLT)

We need to respect other people's boundaries and sometimes at the cost of pushing aside our own personal desires or preferences. We all have ideas and preferences for how we'd like to see things get done, but we need to accept the fact that ours aren't always the correct ways to do things. Like I continue to point out, being a leader does not in any way give us license to impose our ideas or ways of doing things on the other team members. There are team leaders, however, who might tell you otherwise, but we must always test the spirits first, because there are also some leaders who are "wolves in sheep's clothing."

Dear friends, do not believe everyone who claims
to speak by the Spirit. You must test them to
see if the spirit they have comes from God. For
there are many false prophets in the world.
—1 John 4:1 (NLT)

Beware of false prophets, which come to you in sheep's
clothing, but inwardly they are ravening wolves.
—Matthew 7:15 (KJV)

I really can't make it much clearer than that. The Bible, which is God's Word, spells it out completely for us. We don't need to look any further for a better explanation, because there isn't one. We all really need to be more discerning when interacting with others. We also need to make more time to spend in the Word of God, myself included. Because the more time we spend with God, and not just by reading His Word, but also in prayer and private conversations with Him, the more our minds become like Christ's. Living by the fruit of the Spirit will become second nature for us.

All the ways of a man are clean in his own
sight, But the LORD weighs the motives.
—Proverbs 16:2 (NASB)

The church blurred the lines between social boundaries—always a risky business in ancient societies—by bringing together men, women, Greeks, Jews, the wealthy, and the commoners. Powerful people rarely look kindly on such things.
—Chris Tiegreen

CHAPTER 7

Shoulder to Shoulder

Then Moses spoke to the LORD, saying, "May the
LORD, the God of the spirits of all flesh, appoint
a man over the congregation, who will go out and
come in before them, and who will lead them out and
bring them in, so that the congregation of the LORD
will not be like sheep which have no shepherd."
—Numbers 27:15–17 (NASB)

I know almost nothing about shepherding sheep, but I have picked up little tidbits here and there. From my understanding, in different parts of the world, as it is with almost anything, there are different ways of leading a flock. Some lead from the front. Some lead from the rear. Some use hand signals, while others speak to their flocks. But whatever method they use, the sheep know who their shepherd is, and they will follow.

Jesus is a Shepherd even though He is a King. He leads us and His disciples with just two simple words: "Follow Me."

If I haven't made my point yet, I hope to accomplish that in this chapter. After all, this is what this book is about and what inspired me to write it. The title alone should pretty much spell it out for us: *Be a Leader (Be a Shepherd) Not a Ruler (Not a King).*

So how is it that Jesus is a Shepherd and a King? If you haven't read the Bible, then it's a fairly valid question, because that's where you'll find the answer.

You'll Be Sorry

In the opening verses, Moses is addressing God soon before Joshua succeeds him as Israel's leader. Moses, however, wasn't a king. He was their shepherd per se, and so Joshua was as well. Besides the fact that they were a bunch of grumbling complainers, Israel functioned just fine under their leaderships and through a period of judges as well, until one day they decided that they wanted a king so they could be like the other surrounding nations.

> *Then all the elders of Israel gathered together and
> came to Samuel at Ramah; and they said to him,
> "Behold, you have grown old, and your sons do not
> walk in your ways. Now appoint a king for us to judge
> us like all the nations." But the thing was displeasing
> in the sight of Samuel when they said, "Give us a king
> to judge us." And Samuel prayed to the LORD.*
> *—1 Samuel 8:4–6 (NASB)*

God knew that this wasn't a good idea, so through Samuel He warned them against it. The Israelites, however, thought they knew best.

> *Nevertheless, the people refused to listen to the voice of
> Samuel, and they said, "No, but there shall be a king over
> us, that we also may be like all the nations, that our king*

*may judge us and go out before us and fight our battles."
Now after Samuel had heard all the words of the people, he
repeated them in the LORD'S hearing. The LORD said to
Samuel, "Listen to their voice and appoint them a king." So
Samuel said to the men of Israel, "Go every man to his city."*
—1 Samuel 8:19–22 (NASB)

From that day on, all of Israel's kings failed in some way. David, the greatest king of all, sinned horribly. God also never allowed him to rebuild the Temple because there was too much blood shed on his hands. Therefore his son Solomon, the wisest king of all, was chosen by God to do the rebuilding. But then, even he was led away from God and worshiped pagan gods.

Nebuchadnezzar, the king of Babylon, could have been one of the greatest kings, had his own pride not gotten in the way. Josiah became the king when he was just eight years old and came close to living a sinless life. He destroyed pagan worship and reinstated the Mosaic laws. He also celebrated a Passover that was more spectacular than any since the days of Samuel the prophet. But his demise came when he failed to heed King Neco's peaceful warning from God not to go into battle. He disguised himself and went out anyway, and he ended up being shot dead by Egyptian archers (see 2 Chronicles 35:20–24).

The list of kings can go on and on, from the Old Testament to the New Testament. As Mark Clark points out in his book *The Problem of God*, the Bible gives us examples not only of how to live but how not to live by using kings as examples. So no matter how hard we look for a successful king in the Bible, we will find that they all failed in some way, except for one. Jesus.

Pride

Whether the kings of the Bible lived by God's word or not, they all had one thing in common—pride—and that's what did them all in. It's not impossible to live a life free of pride; however, it usually is extremely difficult, and all of us are guilty of it at some point. We may only exhibit our pride very few times throughout our physical lives. But when it does rear its ugly head, we need to be aware of it, so that we can control it and humble ourselves. Because not only are we displaying our pride to others, but we also display it to God, and God hates pride.

It's easy as a leader of anything to let pride lead us too. Because when we're in charge of something, especially if we're new at it, our authority can go to our heads. That's when we allow pride to lead us instead of allowing God to lead us. And once again, as leaders, we need to be setting good examples for others to follow. And keep in mind that not only does pride come from the enemy, but it's also a sin. A deadly sin.

Pride goeth before destruction, and an
haughty spirit before a fall.
—Proverbs 16:18 (KJV)

And he gives grace generously. As the Scriptures say,
"God opposes the proud but gives grace to the humble."
—James 4:6 (NLT)

Sinless

Jesus is the only King to live a completely pure and sinless life, not only because we need a pure, unblemished Lamb to atone for our sins, but also because He is God, and God does not sin. From the very beginning of His human life to the end, He remained sinless. He was born of a virgin, so He began pure. He served man by His healing and also by performing miracles, but He never did anything for Himself. He never asked us for anything, and He gave everything, including His life. Therefore, He was the Perfect Lamb. He died for our sins, and not for His, because He has none.

And when He rose up victoriously from the grave, Satan, sin, and death were all defeated so we can live in His victory. Forty days later, He returned to His home in Heaven, and He now sits on His throne—at the Father's right hand until the day that He returns to take us home.

> *There is more than enough room in my Father's home. If this were not so, would I have told you that I am going to prepare a place for you?*
> *—John 14:2 (NLT)*

King or Shepherd?

Jesus is the fulfillment of the Scriptures, and He frequently quoted verses about Himself, yet nobody truly understood or believed Him until he rose to life again and ascended into Heaven. And during His ministry here on Earth, He led His twelve disciples shoulder to shoulder as a shepherd, and they called Him Master. He washed their feet, and yet they bowed at His. He taught with authority but never from a pedestal or a throne. And now, He sits high upon His throne, the King of all kings.

So yes, Jesus is a true King and He is a true Shepherd. He leads, and we follow. He rules, and we obey. Well, we try to anyway, and that's why it was necessary for Him to come to Earth to give us the free gifts of forgiveness and salvation, because we could have never earned them on our own. So even though He is our King, He came to be our Shepherd and to lead us home.

Just a Baby

Even when He was a newborn baby, angels sang out with songs of great joy over Him. Wise men journeyed over great distances to bring Him gifts. Shepherds bowed before His cradle. People from all walks of life came to worship the Newborn King. And some kings were so threatened by Him that one even sought His life. And why all the fuss? This Newborn King, who was just a baby, is the Savior of the world, the Savior of all mankind.

And she gave birth to a son, a male child, who is to-rule all the-nations with a rod of iron; and her child was caught up to God and to His throne.
—Revelation 12:5 (NASB)

Lead the Flock

If you're the leader of a church band or of any other ministry, the team, or the flock if you will, expects you to do exactly that—*lead*. They look up to you. They submit to you and obey whatever you ask them to do. You don't need to be bossy. You don't need to be arrogant. You don't need to be condescending. All you need to do is ask nicely and politely, and they will obey. Why? It's simple. Because you are their leader. And by you being their leader, they automatically know that they must submit to you, so they will.

You should never say to any member of the team that they have to submit to you. You should never call for mandatory meetings. Jesus never leads from a pedestal, so you shouldn't either. Jesus leads shoulder to shoulder, as should you. The word *leader* implies all these things. So to do otherwise shows lack of self-esteem on your part, and the team will lose confidence in your ability to lead. A true leader acts like a leader. A true leader acts like a shepherd. A king isn't a true leader unless He goes by the name of Jesus. A king is like a child or a teenager with too much authority.

And yes, Jesus was a King as a baby. He was a King as a child. He was a King as a teenager. He was a King as a man. He is still a King today, and He is our King forever. He is also our Shepherd forever, so follow Him, be like Him, and don't take your eyes off Him.

> *So they got in the boat and went off to a remote place by themselves. Someone saw them going and the word got around. From the surrounding towns people went out on foot, running, and got there ahead of them. When Jesus arrived, he saw this huge crowd. At the sight of them, his heart broke—like sheep with no shepherd they were. He went right to work teaching them.*
> —Mark 6:32–34 (MSG)

Be Humble

Prior to their failures, all the great kings were successful because of their humility. For example, when asked by God what he desired, King Solomon asked for wisdom and understanding. This was very pleasing to God, so He did grant Solomon's request. God also gave him great riches and honor (see 1 Kings 3:5–14).

Nobody likes a leader who thinks he or she is more important than the other members of the team simply because he or she is the leader. You need to remember that without all the other members, there would be no team. Therefore, everybody is equally important.

> *If one part suffers, every part suffers with it; if one*
> *part is honored, every part rejoices with it.*
> *—1 Corinthians 12:26 (NIV)*

In Matthew 20:16, Jesus also made it very clear to us that the last will be first and the first will be last.

Children, Adults, Everybody

Growing up, I often heard the saying "Children should be seen but not heard." Jesus, however, placed a higher importance on children than I was raised to believe they have. I always felt inferior to our adults because of such comments. While I do understand, and did back then, that we should respect our elders, that does not make children any less important than adults. It only puts them in a lesser role of authority. Jesus is very clear on this point as well.

> *Then some children were brought to Him so that He*
> *might lay His hands on them and pray; and the disciples*
> *rebuked them. But Jesus said, "Let the children alone,*
> *and do not hinder them from coming to Me; for the*
> *kingdom of heaven belongs to such as these."*
> *—Matthew 19:13–14 (NASB)*

The Bible is also very clear about respecting our elders and also respecting everyone else. The bottom line is being a leader does not make us any more important than anyone else. It only puts us in a position to lead, and not to rule, so we should lead shoulder to shoulder.

> *Do not sharply rebuke an older man, but rather appeal to him*
> *as a father, to the younger men as brothers, the older women*
> *as mothers, and the younger women as sisters, in all purity.*
> *—1 Timothy 5:1–2 (NASB)*

Don't Patronize

There will be times when we need to speak to a member in private about something of a sensitive nature, perhaps about improving on a certain aspect of his or her performance. This can also be awkward for both of you, so you need to be gentle when presenting such subject matter. You might begin with compliments and point out what you do like about what he or she is doing, which is good. But whatever you do, don't pour it on too thick, especially when you are speaking to somebody who is an expert at reading people. And how would you know something like that? Chapter 1, "Know Their Story." If you are falsely pumping a person up just to lighten the blow of bad news, your pupils will be dilating off the charts. Yes, they will.

Start with a couple of quick, genuine compliments, and then just get right to the point. Because right away when you ask to speak to somebody, human nature will automatically make the person think it's bad news anyway, so he or she is probably not even paying attention to the compliments. That person is more than likely thinking about what could possibly be wrong and trying to figure out why you wanted to speak to him or her in the first place. Therefore, you're always better off if you just get straight to it. And most importantly, be honest—absolutely honest. If you're not, there's always that possibility that it could spell trouble for you down the road, because nobody likes deception, and the truth always finds its way to the surface.

So once again, and I'll keep stressing this point over and over, be a shepherd, not a king. If you truly want respect from the other team members, you must first—yes, *first*—respect them.

*For the teraphim speak iniquity, And the diviners see
lying visions And tell false dreams; They comfort in
vain. Therefore the people wander like sheep, They
are afflicted, because there is no shepherd.*
—*Zechariah 10:2 (NASB)*

Humble to the End

Jesus came and lived among us through His humble birth. Then
thirty-three years later, He entered Jerusalem triumphantly, yet
He entered humbly on a donkey. His human life came to its end
on the Cross, a humiliating and excruciatingly painful death,
which is reserved mainly for criminals. He did it willingly. And
He did it for us so that we wouldn't have to.

I find it fitting that I'm completing this chapter on Christmas
Eve, because the following quote is from a devotion I read this
morning.

The tidings of Christ's birth echoed in the skies as the
angel of the Lord proclaimed the good news to the lowly
shepherds. Do you think it strange that this glad word was
not first given to the priests, the scholars, or the Pharisees?
The reason is clear: God speaks to those who are prepared
in their hearts to listen. Apparently these humble shepherds
were prepared and therefore able to discern the voice
from Heaven above the noisy din of Earth's confusion.
—Billy Graham

CHAPTER 8

───── ❧ ─────

Don't Be a Teenager

*The leaders of Israel summoned him, and Jeroboam and
the whole assembly of Israel went to speak with Rehoboam.
"Your father was a hard master," they said. "Lighten the
harsh labor demands and heavy taxes that your father
imposed on us. Then we will be your loyal subjects."*
—*1 Kings 12:3–4 (NLT)*

*Then King Rehoboam discussed the matter with the older
men who had counseled his father, Solomon. "What is
your advice?" he asked. "How should I answer these
people?" The older counselors replied, "If you are
willing to be a servant to these people today and give
them a favorable answer, they will always be your loyal
subjects." But Rehoboam rejected the advice of the older
men and instead asked the opinion of the young men who
had grown up with him and were now his advisers.*
—*1 Kings 12:6–8 (NLT)*

*The young men replied, "This is what you should
tell those complainers who want a lighter burden:
'My little finger is thicker than my father's waist!
Yes, my father laid heavy burdens on you, but I'm
going to make them even heavier! My father beat you
with whips, but I will beat you with scorpions!'"*
—*1 Kings 12:10–11 (NLT)*

I'm not sure where this saying originated, but we joke about it at work while interviewing and hiring people. We'll say, "Let's hire some teenagers while they still know everything." I will admit that not only did I have that mentality as a teenager, but I'm still guilty of it at times. In fact, I've actually been told that I'm arrogant, and it has caused me to pay more attention to what I'm saying and how I'm saying it. From it, I've also found that it can be difficult to earn back another person's respect once you've lost it, so it truly is best if we admit when we're not sure about something or simply just don't know.

Occasionally, I'm required to train young people at work, and I've found it to be very frustrating. They don't seem to stay focused on what I'm trying to teach them. They look around the office, talk to people walking by, and constantly interrupt to tell me how to do it. Then almost always without fail, each time I give them a practice assignment, it's not quite right. I'll ask how they did it. And when I say, "But I showed you the way to do it," I'll get a response along the lines of "I know that's how you showed me, but I wanted to try it my way." So I'll ask them to try again, but the way I showed them, and sometimes I get the same result. Then I have to actually show them why their way doesn't work.

*A fool utters all his mind, but a wise man
keeps it in until afterwards.*
—Proverbs 29:11 (MEV)

The younger generation seems to be out to prove everybody else wrong and that they know more than everybody. They'll go as far as to do something completely opposite from a method that has already been proven to work and work well. An example I can give is running. I have been told by younger people that I no longer need to stretch before I run because it's "old school." However, if I don't stretch before I run and walk myself down when I finish, I either injure myself or I'm in pain all day afterward.

Perhaps the human body has changed since I began running forty-eight years ago, but I've always needed to stretch first, and I still do.

The Voice of Experience

King Rehoboam began with the right idea. When the people came to him with their request, he went directly to older and wiser men with experience for advice. And in verse 7, they told him the people would always be his loyal subjects if he answered them favorably. Other translations say, "Then they will be your servants forever." Now I don't know about you, but that sounds like pretty good advice to me. So what did he do? He decided that wasn't good enough for him, so he went to his younger know-it-all buddies hoping they would tell him what he wanted to hear. And that's exactly what they did. He took their advice instead of the advice of the older, wiser, more experienced men. As you can see, it was quite the opposite.

So what happened next? The kingdom became divided, followed by three hundred years of civil war. And the throne was eventually torn away from his family. Where do you think he went wrong?

And beheld among the simple ones, I discerned among the youths, a young man void of understanding.
—*Proverbs 7:7 (KJV)*

Do You Really Know It All?
Let's suppose you're a fairly new leader for the music team, and there are a few members of that team whose individual musical experience surpasses the total years you've even been alive. That can be quite intimidating, but this is your chance to learn humility, especially if you're the type to butt heads. Because if they have courage enough to tell you, as the leader, that you may not be correct about something, it's extremely likely that you're not.

Now I'm not saying that the older folks are always right. However, they have been around the block a few more times than you have, and there's a good chance they've already experienced whatever it is that you insist on being right about. So the best advice I can give you to start with is the following:

- Listen to what they have to say, and be open-minded.
- Don't be too quick to disagree.
- Do your research so you don't make a fool of yourself.
- Do not be stubborn or unreasonable.
- Seek advice from a former leader if needed.
- Consider the possibility that you could be wrong.

Because as I've already said and will continue to, being a leader by no means makes us automatically right. If somebody has been at this longer than we have, the best thing we can do is to embrace what they have to offer and learn from it.

Don't Impose

As leaders, we may have many ideas that we'd like to implement. But just because they seem logical to us, doesn't necessarily mean that they'll work for everybody. We need to be aware when something isn't working and not force it. A good example, which I had mentioned in chapter 1, is that Coach Bill Belichick builds a game plan around the strengths and the abilities of the players rather than expecting the players to fit into a game plan. We must be able to step back, be willing to admit our ideas may not be the best, and consider suggestions from the other members.

We are appointed as leaders to do just that—*lead*. Being a leader does give us charge over the music team. But in this case, it may be better to pay more attention to the definition of *lead*, which says to guide or direct. After all, this is church. Isn't it? So if you want to tell people what to do and how they should do it, then perhaps you might consider changing your title to "Team King."

> *Trust in the LORD with all your heart, And lean*
> *not on your own understanding; In all your ways*
> *acknowledge Him, And He shall direct your paths.*
> *—Proverbs 3:5–6 (NKJV)*

Be Part of the Team

I'm sure most everybody has heard this cliché before: "There's no 'I' in Team." And once again, I'm not sure where it came from, but I've heard it used many times. It's one thing to think we may know it all, but it's another to take credit for it all. You may have recruited a lot of the members of the team you're on, or you may have coached them, or both. But because you coached or recruited them doesn't give you the right to take credit for a team effort. Without the entire team roster's involvement, the accomplishments of the team couldn't have occurred. And it's highly unlikely that you did it by yourself.

Tom Brady doesn't blame his Patriot teammates when they lose a game. He takes the blame for his own mistakes. And when they win a game, he gives credit to the other players. Why do you think he has such a humble attitude? Because he knows he can't go out there and win a game by himself. On the flip side, he also knows that the entire team contributes to a loss as well, so they win and lose together, as a team.

As church band leaders, most of us take an active part in the live music presentation, so that makes us very much a part of the team. At some point, we had done it under the leadership of another person. So think about how they led you. Did they lead shoulder to shoulder? Or did they lead from a pedestal? I'm guessing shoulder to shoulder. Because they may not have lasted long as a leader had they done otherwise. So help the team by being part of it. Help others to learn and grow, but also allow others to help you learn and grow.

Iron sharpens iron, So one man sharpens another.
—Proverbs 27:17 (NASB)

Take Responsibility
If we're so eager to take credit for what others have done, then we should be just as willing to take a fall when others fail. Even if you don't follow sports, think about it. How many times do we hear in the news about the head coach of a major sports team getting fired after a losing season? That doesn't always seem fair now. Does it? Shouldn't they fire the entire team?

But would that have been any more justified than firing just the coach? We could probably start a great debate over this, but the reason I think they do that is because it's a lot easier to replace one person than an entire team. The team may also have several talented players, and the coach simply didn't use their skills effectively.

So when things aren't going so well with the team, for whatever reason, be willing to step up to the plate and take responsibility. As leaders, we'll hear praise from other people when the team sounds great, and we're all too willing to accept it. So we must be equally willing to accept it when the team isn't sounding its best. We are leaders. Therefore, we need to act like we're leaders, take it on the chin, and take all responsibility, good, bad, or indifferent.

Experience and Maturity

I don't want to confuse experience with maturity because, on the one hand, a person can have many years of experience yet still not be mature. On the other hand, they can have abundant maturity while they may be lacking in experience. There's a fine line that could be drawn here, so I'll try to break it down a little for you.

Experience

This is something that we acquire after many years of learning, practicing, and performing. If we do anything enough, it stands to reason that we get better at it. And if we spend a great deal of time performing with different musical projects, there's almost always a possibility that we could pick up other aspects and styles of music. For example, you may play drums, and the bass player asks you to hold the bass while he or she is fixing something. Then you ask a few questions and that person shows you how to play some simple riffs. Before you know it, you own six basses, and you have joined a Led Zeppelin cover band. I'm not joking either. I've seen it happen.

I think you see my point though. The possibilities are there right in front of you, and you never know where they may lead. It's also likely that you know people who play several instruments. It may be reasonable to assume that they didn't start playing them all on the same day. That takes time, and it comes with many years of experience. While it may help, no amount of experience will guarantee maturity.

> *Teach me good discernment and knowledge,*
> *For I believe in Your commandments.*
> *—Psalm 119:66 (NASB)*

Maturity

Here's where our human nature comes in. We can acquire maturity through our upbringing. We can learn it from trial and error and by making many mistakes throughout our lives. Or we can learn it from observing other people's mistakes. However we learn it, maturity comes from within our hearts. Some of us might need to practice taking every thought captive before acting. Others may need to learn self-control. But both play a big part in our maturity.

An impulsive person, for instance, would need to pay attention to all his or her thoughts and learn to take them captive. In other words, "think before you act."

A person with anger issues, especially someone with a quick temper, would need to learn self-control. And thinking before we act applies here as well.

Maturity can't necessarily be taught to somebody per se,

because it's based on emotion and instinct. There could be learned behavior or several bad habits that we need to overcome first.

Here are what I find to be the major differences:

- Experience is more physical and mental, meaning it comes from actually doing something hands-on and gaining the necessary knowledge and ability to be able to repeat certain tasks.
- Maturity can come from experience; however, it's more a makeup of emotional and psychological instincts. Here, we need to be at peace with God in order to be at peace with ourselves and before we can be at peace with others.

So in a nutshell, experience is based more on knowledge, whereas maturity is based more on wisdom and common sense.

Once again, I will direct your attention back to chapter 3, where we talked about the fruit of the Spirit because it is the Holy Spirit we receive guidance from. And if we open up our eyes, ears, hearts, minds, and souls to Him, He will guide us.

> *Wisdom is with the aged,*
> *and understanding in length of days.*
> *—Job 12:12 (ESV)*

The Cover-Up

What I'm talking about here could be more of an adolescent or teenage mentality. However, adults can be guilty of this as well. If we think of ourselves as inferior to others in some way, we might tend to point out faults in others to draw attention away from what we perceive as our own shortcomings. Joyce

Meyer talks about it in her daily devotional "Battlefield of the Mind." On Day 76, titled "Passing Judgement," she mentions a plump young girl who said terrible things to obese people to do just that.

I can also remember on more than one occasion, a few different front men asking other band members to tone it down so that the audience's attention wouldn't be drawn away from them. That's somewhat the opposite; however, it is the same mentality. In both cases, such behavior is triggered by low self-esteem. One doesn't have confidence enough to receive attention while the other lacks confidence enough to draw attention.

So in taking thoughts captive and living by the fruit of the Spirit, we need to avoid this. We must be accountable for ourselves, and we need to allow others to be accountable for themselves, not only as leaders or Christians, but as people of the human race in general. We must respect all people for who they are, what they are, where they're from, and what they do. To do otherwise would be breaking God's commandments.

And this is his commandment: We must believe
in the name of his Son, Jesus Christ, and love
one another, just as he commanded us.
—1 John 3:23 (NLT)

The first thing that we need to remind ourselves of, in either case, is that God created each and every one of us with a purpose. None of us are any better than anybody else—just as none of us are any worse than anybody else. Therefore, we must all work together just like brothers and sisters in Christ should, shoulder to shoulder. We are all equal in His eyes. We're all His children, and therefore, God loves each of us equally.

*"If you listen to these regulations and faithfully obey them,
the LORD your God will keep his covenant of unfailing love
with you, as he promised with an oath to your ancestors.*
—Deuteronomy 7:12 (NLT)

Be Confident

As leaders, we don't only need to edify others, but we also
need to allow ourselves to be edified by others—although
we need to do so without letting it go to our heads. It is OK
though to be confident. In fact, we should be confident.
And not just the leaders but every member of God's Family
should have confidence in his or her abilities. But we all
need to have confidence in each other as well. This isn't
a competition we're in, so there's absolutely no need at
all to let it bother us if another member of the team has
more experience than we ourselves do. Like I said, and will
continue to say, we need to embrace what other members of
the team have to offer.

Think of it like a Bible study group. We learn and grow
together there, so there's no reason why we can't learn and grow
together in a music ministry, as God's band. When you see your
brother or sister stumbling, go help him or her get back up. If
we ourselves stumble—and yes, leaders do stumble—we need
to swallow our pride and ask for help. When we face our own
needs and then have courage enough to ask for help, it will
make us look stronger than trying to hide our fear makes us
look. And don't forget. The truth always has a way of coming
to the surface, so don't try to hide it.

So don't just lead; be a team player. And when you're called
upon to do so, take one for the team. Think of it this way.

Somebody has enough confidence in your ability to lead, so he or she put you into that role for good reason. That in itself should build up your confidence.

Above all, keep fervent in your love for one another,
because love covers a multitude of sins. Be hospitable
to one another without complaint. As each one has
received a special gift, employ it in serving one another
as good stewards of the manifold grace of God.
—1 Peter 4:8–10 (NASB)

The needs of the many outweigh the
needs of the few, or the one.
—Spock

CHAPTER 9

---⟨∼⟩---

A Later Chapter

*How you have fallen from heaven, morning star, son of the
dawn! You have been cast down to the earth, you who once
laid low the nations! You said in your heart, "I will ascend
to the heavens; I will raise my throne above the stars of God;
I will sit enthroned on the mount of assembly, on the utmost
heights of Mount Zaphon. I will ascend above the tops of the
clouds; I will make myself like the Most High." But you are
brought down to the realm of the dead, to the depths of the
pit. Those who see you stare at you, they ponder your fate:
"Is this the man who shook the earth and made kingdoms
tremble, the man who made the world a wilderness, who
overthrew its cities and would not let his captives go home?"*
—Isaiah 14:12–17 (NIV)

I can remember back in school we always had teachers we
didn't like, and the consensus seemed fairly uniform in most
cases. We would entertain each other by secretly mocking them
with what we thought were funny impersonations. We would
use an exaggerated voice and quote them and sometimes try
to act like them also in an exaggerated manner. There were

also some nice teachers who we liked, but there was never a shortage of those that we poked fun at. There were a few principals we took shots at as well.

Many of our targets earned such disrespect because they acted as though they were above the law. We had a very nasty teacher who we also feared. One day when the class was unattended for a few minutes, the students took advantage of the opportunity to unleash an awful attack on me. And it wasn't just the bullies; it was almost the entire class. I reported this to the teacher upon return. The teacher then began bullying me, and the entire class joined back in, so I ran to the main office and requested that I be removed from that class. The principal put me into another much safer class. From what I understand, the bully teacher was never reprimanded and never stopped bullying.

I went back a few years later when I was bigger, stronger, and had more confidence, seeking to get revenge on that teacher. And when I found the teacher, I was so surprised to see just how small that person actually was. I was also a bit surprised when that teacher started a minor confrontation with me, as if to continue right where we had left off. I actually felt a little sorry for the teacher. But I stood my ground this time and didn't back down. And when the teacher's smile turned into a look of fear, that was good enough for me, so I just walked away.

No Exemptions

Believe it or not, there are some music ministry leaders who lead with the mentality that they're above the law, very much like that bully teacher. They may not attack physically. However, they will try to use what they consider to be acceptable means. And in doing so, they can cause a great many people not to like them. And even though we're Christians, it doesn't prevent us from mocking them like we did those teachers and principals.

OK. Our switchboards just lit up on that one, so let's take the first caller. And we hear, "How dare you say that about Christians? I'm Christian, and I would never do anything like that."

Then suddenly a buzzer sounds. "Oh, I'm sorry. That's not the correct answer." Yeah, I apologize for my warped sense of humor again, but I couldn't resist.

Yes. That's right. Christians do act like that as well. The reason I say that is because I've witnessed it. And don't forget. We were all born physically alive, yet spiritually dead until we came to Christ. As I quoted Neil Anderson in the first chapter, "We don't have an instant delete button," so we all have bad habits that we need to break. Some might take a long time to overcome, and Satan will have a field day with that. So we all must be fully aware of how we treat others and learn to humble ourselves.

Leaders

This may not apply to all of us; however, there are some leaders who think they can get away with treating anybody any way they want. And they believe that being a leader gives them the right to do so. They may get away with it at some churches if nobody is complaining about it, but they're not getting away with it with God.

If a leader puts him- or herself above the law and mistreats other members of the team, it causes strife. Sometimes that strife will come out into the open by way of a confrontation or argument. It can be brought to the campus or lead pastor's attention in a formal or informal complaint, or it could become gossip or mocking.

And yes, sometimes it does result in behind-the-back mocking, very much like what I talked about in the opening story. We may not even realize that people are doing this behind our backs because they seem to like us when we're face to face. Sometimes, leaders may exalt themselves to the point where they don't think they can do anything wrong, so they would never suspect anything like this could go on. But believe me, it does. I've seen it, and it's not funny.

Mockers

Nobody should do this, Christian or otherwise. We are all God's children, and we all deserve respect from each other. Period. If a leader infuriates you enough to resort to this type of behavior, you must take proper action before it gets out of hand. I can offer a few suggestions:

- Try speaking to the leader to resolve it.
- Seek advice from a pastor if necessary.
- And if all else fails, file a complaint.
- But do not gossip or mock.

Anger can sometimes take over, but that's where we need to take thoughts captive and live by the fruit of the Spirit.

Wine is a mocker and beer a brawler; whoever is led astray by them is not wise. A king's wrath strikes terror like the roar of a lion; those who anger him forfeit their lives. It is to one's honor to avoid strife, but every fool is quick to quarrel.
—Proverbs 20:1–3 (NIV)

This Is Church

Yes. This is church, and none of us should forget that. We will get into a little more detail about this in the chapter titled "How and Why," but there can never be too much emphasis on this, so I'm touching on it here a little before we move on. We need to focus on "why" we do what we do and worry less about "how" we do it.

We are doing this to serve God and not man or ourselves or anybody else for that matter. The churches do benefit in some way from our work though, so all our leaders, pastors included, need to remember that. It doesn't, however, entitle any of us to get special treatment, but it does entitle us to respectful treatment from our leaders. Why? Because God makes that very clear in all His commandments. Also, Jesus makes it very clear as well.

> *Therefore, whatever you want men to do to you, do also to them, for this is the Law and the Prophets.*
> *—Matthew 7:12 (NKJV)*

Are We Not Volunteers?

I know some leaders may not like this one. However, this is where we need to swallow our pride, humble ourselves, take all thoughts captive, and live by the fruit of the Spirit, specifically self-control.

Right off the bat, the word *volunteer* should automatically put up a red flag. We simply cannot treat any volunteers the same way that we would treat paid employees. We can't impose the same rules on them. We can't impose the same demands. And we certainly need to be well aware of "boundaries" that we cannot encroach upon. We also need to avoid using certain phrases and wording. Here are just a few examples of things not to say:

- This is my team.
  Why? Because it's not your team. It's God's team. You don't own it or anybody on it; therefore, you have no right to call it yours.
- You have to submit to me.
  Why? Because by being leaders, it is implied that the members should submit to us. We should never say it. Period.
- There will be mandatory meetings.
  Why? Because you simply cannot impose this on volunteers. They may vary from state to state, but there are laws regarding this.
- I'm going to make a better _____ out of you.
  Why? Because you can't make a better anything out of anybody. Only God can do that.

And I'm going to explain the last one separately in a little more detail.

The Principal's Office

I have mildly alluded to this a few times, and here I'm referring to the last point about making a better anything out of anybody. If we have any team members who we feel need to improve in some areas, the last thing we want to do is to call them into the back room with another leader and sit them down to talk. This can make somebody very uncomfortable in more ways than one. It can make them feel like they're being ganged up on, or it could make them feel like juvenile delinquents being called into the principal's office.

If this is really necessary, it would be best for everybody to allow the people to bring prayer partners of their choosing. This may put them a little more at ease by making them not feel so outnumbered. Many companies employ this practice, not only for that purpose, but also for legal protection. This way, everybody has a witness so nothing said can be denied later. And yes, some Christian leaders do deny what they say at times. Once again, I have seen it happen. What makes it worse is when the pastors believe the deceptive leader. And yes, that happens too.

You're Not God, Are You?

Under no circumstances should we as leaders tell anybody that we're going to make them better at whatever it is that they do. Because like I said, only God can do that. It's also boasting, which God frowns upon. Here's what most translations of James 4:16 say about boasting: "As it is, you boast in your arrogance. All such boasting is evil." I personally like the NLV translation: "But instead you are proud. You talk loud and big about yourselves. All such pride is sin." It makes you think. Doesn't it?

So to say that we are going to make somebody better at something is the equivalent of elevating ourselves to God's level. And I really don't think I need to remind anybody of what happened to Lucifer when he did that. He was called down to the principal's office, and he was suspended from school for a very long time.

So the great dragon was cast out, that serpent of old, called the Devil and Satan, who deceives the whole world; he was cast to the earth, and his angels were cast out with him.
—Revelation 12:9 (NKJV)

Improvement Program

Now let's say you explain to the person you would like him or her to take part in an improvement program. First of all, anybody who has worked in management knows that it's only a polite way of telling a member that they're off the team. Companies will do a similar thing when they have any employees they want to get rid of, but they have no legal means to fire them, so they will put them into such a program. And no matter how much they improve, it doesn't make any difference because the employers have already decided that they don't want them working there anymore. It has become a legal means of firing people without having a reason.

So if a music team leader asks you to take part in an improvement program, it more than likely means that you will be off the team at the end of the allotted time. How do I know this? You guessed it. I have seen this happen as well. In fact, I've actually witnessed a music team member being set up for failure in a so-called improvement program.

The team leader explained to that person that there were certain aspects of his or her playing that needed to change or stop altogether, which just happened to be that person's natural mannerisms. And as part of the improvement program, he or she was asked to watch videos of Christian drummers whose styles were preferred. Then the person was expected to copy them. When that person watched all the videos, the drummers in the videos were doing the same things that team drummer was asked to stop or change. So as it turned out, that drummer was set up for failure. To top it off, that person never got the review that was promised at the completion of the program. He or she was also left off the service schedule without any explanation. So as you can see, that program was nothing more than a ruse to get that person off the music team.

It really hurts me to say this, but, yes, this sort of thing does go on in churches. So being a Christian, a volunteer, and even a member of God's Family doesn't prevent stuff like this from going on. Satan is out there, and his soldiers are infiltrating our churches by taking leadership positions and driving a wedge between us in an attempt to stunt the growth of God's Kingdom. We need to be vigilant and discerning in order to protect ourselves and each other from such deception.

but we have renounced the things hidden because of shame, not walking in craftiness or adulterating the word of God, but by the manifestation of truth commending ourselves to every man's conscience in the sight of God.
—2 Corinthians 4:2 (NASB)

Reality Sets In

I know a lot of this sounds a bit shocking, especially when we hear about this sort of evil going on at Christian churches. However, it is very real, and it does indeed go on. There are very many leaders who think so highly of themselves that they'll implement whatever rules they want and expect everybody on the team to follow them regardless of how much it imposes on people's personal lives or how it affects them emotionally. They simply don't care how insulting or demeaning their treatment of others can be, because they actually believe that by being a leader, they have the right to do whatever they want.

And if you don't agree, may I remind you about the sexual

abuse scandals that have been all over the news? In fact, some of those cases are still ongoing. So if something that horrible can go on in a church, then what's to prevent stuff like phony improvement programs from happening? Nothing. That's right. Nothing.

Perhaps nothing can completely prevent it from happening, but when it does, our pastors need to act, and act quickly. Because the longer we delay at fixing such problems, the bigger they will get, and the more people will be hurt by it. Not only will members of the church be hurt, but the church can suffer as well. If news of such treatment spreads throughout the church, people are going to become upset and possibly leave the church. So let's face it. Would you want to be a member at a church where team leaders are allowed to treat team members in such a disrespectful way?

Don't let anyone deceive you in any way, for that day will not come until the rebellion occurs and the man of lawlessness is revealed, the man doomed to destruction. He will oppose and will exalt himself over everything that is called God or is worshiped, so that he sets himself up in God's temple, proclaiming himself to be God. Don't you remember that when I was with you I used to tell you these things? And now you know what is holding him back, so that he may be revealed at the proper time. For the secret power of lawlessness is already at work; but the one who now holds it back will continue to do so till he is taken out of the way. And then the lawless one will be revealed, whom the Lord Jesus will overthrow with the breath of his mouth and destroy by the splendor of his coming.
—2 Thessalonians 2:3–8 (NIV)

Paul and the other apostles warned the churches of evil deception, false teachers, and false prophets a couple thousand years ago. So, how much do you think has actually changed since then? I think you know the answer.

It's time to take off the gloves, rip off the masks, knock off the rationalizations, and face the truth head-on.
—Charles R. Swindoll

CHAPTER 10

Deception at Work

Her leaders in it are like wolves tearing up the prey to shed blood and destroy people, in order to benefit unjustly.
—Ezekiel 22:27 (CJB)

For such men are false apostles, deceitful workers, disguising themselves as apostles of Christ. No wonder, for even Satan disguises himself as an angel of light. Therefore it is not surprising if his servants also disguise themselves as servants of righteousness, whose end will be according to their deeds.
—2 Corinthians 11:13–15 (NASB)

I was raised Eastern Orthodox and attended Sunday school, and I didn't like it much better than regular school. I always wanted to sit upstairs with the adults. I felt as though we weren't being told the truth or that something was being left out, so I thought that I would find the answers upstairs. Well, I was right about one thing. The answers are upstairs—way Upstairs. And the good news is we don't have to wait until we get *There* to know them either, because they're all written out for us in the Bible.

Jesus said to the people who believed in him, "You are truly my disciples if you remain faithful to my teachings. And you will know the truth, and the truth will set you free."
—John 8:31–32 (NLT)

No Safe Haven

One would expect to be able to go to church and be safe. Yes, safe from bullying or from insults or any type of abusive treatment, but I found out at an early age that church is no guarantee of safety. In fact, we see evidence of this to a much greater degree in the news. I never met with that type of abuse, but it was still a bit difficult to accept. As a young child, I was slapped in the face by a priest for not kissing his hand while receiving Communion. And as an adult, I was the butt-end of a priest's joke for my religious upbringing.

I know that these are only minor incidents in comparison to what we all hear about in the news, but it's still not the kind of treatment anybody would expect to get from any priest of any denomination. Our priests, pastors, rabbis, or any and all clergy are the very ones we should feel safe turning to for help. And we should be able to turn to them without worrying about how they're going to judge us or treat us. They're there to teach us, protect us, and set for us good examples, examples that glorify God's Kingdom. They're the ones we would expect to be living by the fruit of the Spirit.

Chain of Command

Of course, when a problem arises in a church, the first person we should turn to is the leader of the ministry that we're a member of. If that leader can't help or won't help, or perhaps is even the cause of the problem, then we need to take it to a higher level. Although it's always preferable to resolve it with that leader first, it's not always possible. That's when we may need to turn to a higher authority.

Many churches have a campus pastor who serves several functions within the church. This is the person you would want to consider speaking to if this option is available. If not, you can discreetly ask a leader from another ministry to suggest someone you could take a certain matter to. That leader may be able to get you heading in the right direction. And if you can, avoid bringing it to the lead pastor or the person in charge. He or she has much more important things to worry about, so this should only be a last resort, which is precisely why many churches have a campus pastor. Unless the lead pastor is the person who would handle such a problem, try not to bother him or her.

> *But now Jesus, our High Priest, has been given a*
> *ministry that is far superior to the old priesthood,*
> *for he is the one who mediates for us a far better*
> *covenant with God, based on better promises.*
> *—Hebrews 8:6 (NLT)*

Alone in the World

Sometimes, I like to be alone, and sometimes, I don't. But when I am, I don't necessarily feel as though I am. I live in the town I grew up in, so I see friends fairly often, and I have a cousin who lives only five minutes away, but this wasn't always the case. I had lived up in the Lowell, Massachusetts, area for twenty years. Besides my neighbors, my closest friend or relative was about a half hour away. I know that's not really far, and it didn't bother me until I was very ill and lying on my couch for a few months, which was difficult for me because I'm an extremely active person. It did, however, make me think a lot, and one thing that kept coming to mind was how alone I really was. In the entire time I lived there, I only had three unexpected visits from friends. I had that many my first week back here in Holliston. I was less than an hour from here, and yet I started becoming homesick, and that's when I decided it was time to come home.

During the past six-plus years, I've come to Christ and have been attending church regularly. I've read several Christian books, and I read the entire Bible each year. I've joined a few Bible studies and continue to lead Bible study groups. From all that I've learned in this time, one of the most important things I want to share with you is that we are never alone. I'm not. You're not. Nobody is.

God is with each and every one of us. He might not always make His Presence known to us, but He's there, and He most certainly wants us to know that. All we need to do is ask. Yes, that's it. Just ask. Invite Him into your life. Ask Him to come closer. Tell Him that you want to have a relationship with Him. Because that's what He wants. All we have to do is ask. James 4:8 (NLT) says it best: "Come close to God, and God will come close to you."

Alone in the Church
Although God is always with us, we can't depend on people to be with us like He is. Sometimes, when we face certain situations, we can feel very, very much alone, no matter how many people are around. The drummer that I had mentioned in chapter 9 is a perfect example of someone who felt very much alone in church. After being placed into a so-called improvement program, allegedly for lack of skills, that person

never received the review that was promised and was also left off the service schedule without any explanation. As it turned out, there really was no explanation or review because it was all just a ruse, as I also mentioned, to get that person off the team. We'll get into more detail about that in chapter 11, "How and Why." But what do you think about this? Deception perhaps?

This is the type of situation I was talking about when I mentioned that the leader could possibly be the cause of the problem, and here that certainly was the case. From what I understand, there was absolutely no reasoning with that leader, so the problem needed to be taken to a higher level of authority. The problem is, everybody turned out to be in on it. Now what do you think? Deception across the board perhaps?

It truly is sad when you turn to a pastor for help, to a person you thought was your friend, a person you thought you could trust, only to get thrown under the bus. Now that's turning the other cheek a couple times over. Wouldn't you say?

Through his skill he'll cause deceit to prosper under his leadership. He'll promote himself and will destroy many while they are secure. He'll take a stand against the Prince of Princes, yet he'll be crushed without human help.
—Daniel 8:25 (ISV)

Sad but True

It's very unfortunate when deception of any kind goes on within a church. And as I mentioned in the opening to this chapter, church should be a place where we can go to and feel safe. Not only should we *feel* safe, but we absolutely should *be* safe, not just from bullying, but also from deception. It doesn't matter what level of leadership somebody is at, nobody should be allowed to use any kind of deception in a church, or anywhere for that matter. And they most certainly should not abuse their authority in any way.

Unfortunately, this sort of thing does go on in churches, and some leaders and pastors are getting away with it. This doesn't mean we all need to become suspicious of the church we belong to or of its leaders. It simply means that if something like this does manifest itself, we should try to stop it before it gets out of control or before it creates an unhealthy environment for the true believers.

If it's a case where it's only in lower levels of leadership and it's being conducted in a way as to keep the higher-ups from knowing about it, then we need to go directly to the front office or whoever is at the top of the chain of command. If the front office is unaware of such activity, they need to know about it immediately so that appropriate action can be taken. It's not all that uncommon for team leaders to think they can get away with almost anything. Their authority can go to their heads, and that's when the enemy will step in with his deceptive influence. In that case, that person will need help with the battle for his or her mind, along with being removed from leadership before the problem can grow out of control.

If, however, it's a case where the deception goes right to the top, and the pastors are in on it, then there is nothing that can be done about it. That church isn't there for God or Jesus. They may just be there for business reasons, or it could be a cult of some sort. In either case, you need to leave and find a church that truly does believe in the Bible and worships God and Jesus. They do exist. Believe me. I used to be part of one.

Voices

The first thing we need to consider is the frame of mind of the leader in question.

- Was he or she at one time an honest person?
- Is he or she a true believer?
- Is he or she on an ego trip?
- Is he or she easily intimidated by people who have more experience?
- How does the leader respond when you call him or her out on dishonest or inaccurate statements?
- Is he or she listening to the wrong voice?

These are a few examples of psychological or spiritual questions you need to explore in order to understand why a leader would be using deception in the first place. Every Christian is in an ongoing battle for his or her mind, so he or she could be hearing as many as three or more voices all at one time, depending on how many demons are present, but let's break it down to a few main ones.

First, we have our own voice, which comes from our own personal thoughts. They are influenced by many things, such as upbringing, education, work experience, peer pressure, media, and anything that has had some effect on how we think. This voice could be all over the place, which is exactly why we need to take all our thoughts captive in obedience to Christ (2 Corinthians 10:5). We also need to discern the good from the bad and act in a way that is pleasing to God. We need to live by the fruit of the Spirit, but we can't do that unless we're listening to the right voice.

The right voice is obviously from God. It can sound like our own voice, and it's in complete agreement with the Scriptures.

He will never say anything bad or negative about us or to us or about anybody. God loves us and will only say words to edify us. Most of the time, His voice will come in the form of Scripture. After all, the Scriptures are God's Words. So needless to say, we will never go wrong by listening to His voice.

Then there's the wrong voice, or sometimes voices. This is where it can get a little tricky. Because, remember, Satan and his clan can be extremely clever. He will never intentionally make his presence known. He's more likely to use words like *I*, *me*, or *my* and disguise his voice to make us think it's our own thoughts. He will even quote Scripture, but he will twist it around in a way to make you second-guess it or yourself. He'll also word it in such a way to make us believe that it doesn't apply to us, so we need to test the spirits.

> *My dear friends, many false prophets are in the world now. So don't believe every spirit, but test the spirits to see if they are from God.*
> —1 John 4:1 (ERV)

The Lost Word

Deception has, unfortunately, become a way of life or a standard of living, if you will. And what I mean by that is just turn on a TV or open a newspaper or any magazine. Not a single one of them can function without some sort of funding. And where do they get the funding? It could come in the form of donations, but the largest source is advertisement. There are ads on just about every page of any newspaper or magazine. And the bigger the ad, the more sponsors pay for that space. On TV, how often do you see commercials? Fairly often. Like the printed ads, the longer they are, the more money they bring in.

To put that in perspective, let's take an NFL game for example. A game consists of four quarters, each lasting fifteen minutes, which totals one hour. Now has anybody ever watched an entire game in real time that lasted for an hour? No. And why do you suppose that is? Commercials and timeouts can add as many as two or more hours to each game. And if you were to time it to see how much of that is actual playing time, it's usually right around fifteen minutes, give or take. News and regular programing aren't much different either.

I apologize for going off on a tangent, but I can get a little carried away sometimes. Anyway, the point that I started to make is how much truth is there to those ads and commercials? Not much. They use so much deception that it's not even funny. And the worst part of it is, we all fall for it. Why? It's because they use clever catchphrases and good-looking people in order to appeal to our senses so that we will want to buy their products.

Does this sound familiar? Well, it should, because that's the same tactic Satan uses. First comes the deception, then he hits us with temptation, and then he finishes us off with the accusations. And that's what our society has become: Satan's playground. We are in the world, and the world is getting into us, just like a boat. It's OK for a boat to be in the water, but you don't want the water getting into the boat, and we don't want the world getting into us.

God's Word, the Bible, has been falling on deaf ears and viewed by blind eyes for so long now that deception has become second nature for our society. It has gotten so bad that it has even seeped its way into our churches. Satan was defeated by Jesus, but you'd never know it by the way we live and how we treat each other. And, yes, I include myself in this, so please don't start finger-pointing. We're all guilty, every single one of us.

*Every one of them has turned aside; They have together
become corrupt; There is none who does good, No, not one.*
                                    —Psalm 53:3 (NKJV)

So now you may be wondering, if I'm including myself and
if I'm just as guilty as everybody else, then why am I calling
everybody out on this? Because I admit when I'm wrong or
make a mistake. We all make mistakes, and we're all wrong on
occasion. Can you look into the mirror and admit when you're
wrong or that you've made a mistake? Truthfully? Think before
you answer. Because God knows the truth, and the truth always
comes out of hiding.

The Weapon

I believe it was Neil Anderson who had asked a former high
priest of Satanism what he considered the greatest weapon
for battling the kingdom of darkness. And his answer was
prayer. Six years ago, I may not have agreed with that,
but I do now. Satan and all his demons absolutely hate it
whenever we pray, and I found this out for myself just a few
months ago.

I was kneeling next to my bed praying, as I do every night
before I go to bed. Most of the time, the light is on, but this was
a rare occasion when I had it off. I was barely a minute into
prayer when I heard a voice in the room, no more than a couple
of feet away from me, and it said, "Shut up." It was an angry-
sounding gravelly male voice, so I stopped and turned in that
direction. I couldn't see in the darkness, but I said, "I can hear
you." Just then, every hair on the back of my neck stood up,
and I could sense the evil presence, so I redirected my prayer
and commanded it to leave, in Jesus' name. The peacefulness

returned, and I finished praying and went right to sleep. I guess he didn't like my prayer. Oh well.

So yes, prayer is our most powerful weapon. It's also the seventh piece of "the Armor of God." In fact, after giving his instructions for putting on the other six pieces of armor, Paul said, "Pray in the Spirit at all times and on every occasion" (Ephesians 6:18 NLT). Satan and his cohorts are intelligent and clever, but they can still become frustrated and flustered. They've just had a few thousand more years than we have to practice hiding their emotions. So no matter what the voices are saying, and no matter what temptations or deceptions are thrown at you, keep praying and don't quit. Oh yes, Satan hears you and so does God, so don't ever stop praying, because Satan hates it and God loves it. Therefore, always, "pray without ceasing" (1 Thessalonians 5:17 NASB).

You could try to use tanks, grenades, or missiles, but none of it will help. In fact, you may only end up inflicting more injury on yourself, because our fight is in the spiritual realm. So as long as you have confessed and truly believe that Christ is your Lord and Savior, Satan and friends must submit to whatever you command them in Jesus' name.

And the seventy returned again with joy, saying, Lord, even the devils are subject unto us through thy name.
—Luke 10:17 (KJV)

For our struggle is not against flesh and blood, but against the rulers, against the authorities, against the powers of this dark world and against the spiritual forces of evil in the heavenly realms.
—Ephesians 6:12 (NIV)

And though it may seem like we're battling humans when we're up against an unruly church leader, it's deception from the enemy. Lucifer and his fallen angels will use any trick in the book to slow down the growth of God's Kingdom. They know they can't stop it. But if they can get us to fall for their lies, they can slow us down. They won't always come as a voice in the darkness. They're way too clever for that, so they will use whatever means they must to get our attention and earn our trust so that we might listen to them. We hate to admit it, but more often than not, they will come to us in the form of a church leader, somebody we believe that we should be able to trust—somebody pretending to be a friend.

We use God's mighty weapons, not worldly weapons, to knock down the strongholds of human reasoning and to destroy false arguments. We destroy every proud obstacle that keeps people from knowing God. We capture their rebellious thoughts and teach them to obey Christ.
—2 Corinthians 10:4–5 (NLT)

Beware of Christian leaders who appear to be very religious by their actions, but who are really glorifying themselves rather than the Lord. We should never honor anyone above God. Only He is truly worthy of our praise.
—Charles F. Stanley

CHAPTER 11

How and Why

"Your words have been arrogant against Me," says the
LORD. "Yet you say, 'What have we spoken against You?'
You have said, 'It is vain to serve God; and what profit
is it that we have kept His charge, and that we have
walked in mourning before the LORD of hosts? So now
we call the arrogant blessed; not only are the doers of
wickedness built up but they also test God and escape.'"
—Malachi 3:13–15 (NASB)

When I began attending a Christian church, I was what they called a "frequent flier." I was there almost every Sunday, but I wasn't really there. And what I mean by that is, I was there physically but not spiritually. This went on for about a year, and then a friend gave me a copy of *The Purpose Driven Life* by Rick Warren, which is a book I highly recommend everybody to read. After reading it, I thought a lot of it made sense, but I felt like I missed something, so I read it again. And that's when it began to sink in. After service the following Sunday, I inquired about becoming a member at that church. As luck would have it, they were offering a class that evening, so I signed up. Then to become a member of the serving team, I needed to attend classes for the next two Sundays, so I did.

Before I completed the classes, I also signed up for my first Bible study group. It was during the summer semester when all the small groups participated in "Serve Day," where each group would volunteer to serve the community in some way. The group that I joined was doing a free car wash at the church parking lot.

I had done volunteer work for churches prior to this, but I always did it with a different mind-set than what came upon me that day. I used to think that I was doing it for the people who were benefiting from it, which I was, but it never occurred to me that I was doing it for God. I also liked drawing attention to the fact that I served as if to pat myself on the back. And, in fact, that's exactly what I was doing, patting myself on the back.

So at the car wash, I was assigned to parking duty, which really was quite fun. While I was standing there waiting for cars to arrive, I looked around at everybody doing their jobs and having fun. Then I thought about what I was doing, and that's when it hit me. Yes. We were serving the people of our community. But most importantly, we were doing it to serve God in order to glorify His Kingdom. That's when the floodgates opened right up, and I began bawling my eyes out.

Why

I want to begin here because "why" is the most important reason for serving. As I mentioned in the opening, we do it to serve God. Then why do others benefit from our work or donations? Please forgive me if this is a long-winded answer, but the way I would put it is like this: We give back to God what already belongs to Him, because He owns everything. He provides for us what we will need for our daily provisions, as stated in the Lord's Prayer: "Give us this day our daily bread." (Matthew 6:11 NASB). So when we give to God, we are giving back to Him what He has already given to us. Therefore, we don't actually own anything. We only borrow what we have from God for as long as we need it. And when we give it back to God, He provides it for those who are in greater need for it than we are, because He knows what each one of us needs before we even know or ask for it.

And since God is the One who is distributing our donations to the ones in need, His Kingdom is glorified by the work we do. So, that is "why" we serve: to serve God and to glorify His Kingdom. We don't do it to serve man or ourselves. That is why God hates greed, because nothing is ours to begin with.

> "So don't worry about these things, saying, 'What will we eat? What will we drink? What will we wear?' These things dominate the thoughts of unbelievers, but your heavenly Father already knows all your needs. Seek the Kingdom of God above all else, and live righteously, and He will give you everything you need.
> —Matthew 6:31–33 (NLT)

You may now be thinking, *OK, that covers food and many other tangible material needs. But how does it pertain to physical work?* The work we do while serving takes up time. And in most cases, it's our own personal time because many of us are volunteers. One of the best ways to show people how much we care about them is to give of our time. And yes, I did say our time. But is it really our time? No. That also belongs to God. It's ours to borrow, however, it's not ours to keep. But He provides us with the time that we need for any given task. And once we use it, it's gone—gone back to Him to be redistributed.

So you see, even our time is borrowed. Therefore, we're all living on borrowed time—time that is provided by God. What He provides us with, whether it's time, food, clothing, or anything else whatsoever, He also gives us the right to choose what we do with it. Therefore, we must use His time wisely.

We don't have to give anything back to God. We don't have to volunteer our time to serve Him. In fact, we don't even have to do anything He tells us to do. It is, however, in our best interest if we do though. We should give back to Him what belongs to Him. We should volunteer our time to serve Him. We should also do what He tells us to do—everything He tells us to do.

And when we give anything back to God, we must not do it out of obligation or just to avoid going to the fiery lake. We should do it cheerfully and because we want to do it, because God knows our hearts and our thoughts. We may be able to put on a good act and fool a lot of people, but we can't fool God.

Each of you should give what you have decided
in your Heart to give, not reluctantly or under
compulsion, for God loves a cheerful giver.
—2 Corinthians 9:7 (NIV)

How

While the reason why we serve is much more important than how we serve, we still shouldn't overlook how. For example, you may not ask a very shy person who doesn't feel comfortable speaking to strangers to greet people at the main entrance. Or you may not ask somebody with a broken leg who is on crutches to do parking duty. OK, I know that's stretching it a bit, but I think you see my point. Each position in our serving teams requires a certain level of skill, a certain level of know-how, and a certain level of desire to do the job at hand.

In order to get in to a music ministry, it's usually a requirement to pass an audition. It's also not uncommon for some churches to require that we go through a training period, which we also need to pass before we can participate with a live band during a church service. And depending on the church and its policies, it's also not out of the question to be offered a position in some church bands without the customary audition.

For example, I happen to know that the drummer I spoke about in chapters 9 and 10 had such offers from more than one church. One of those music team leaders is also a drummer who sought out that person because of his or her experience and reputation. So you may not be surprised to find out that this person's experience included performing with several national touring acts and a fair amount of studio time. Not to mention that drummer has a reputation for being one of the best in the business for playing with a click track. If you're familiar with church music presentation, then you know how important that is.

So now you might be wondering, *How could a person with those credentials end up in an improvement program?* The answer really is quite simple. As I mentioned in chapter 9, that drummer wasn't wanted on the team, so the team leaders set that person up for failure. It was also suggested that the team's main leader is greatly intimidated by the drummer's experience and doesn't like having anybody on the team who knows when he or she is pretending to know more than he or she actually does know. It's quite possible that the enemy had a hand in it too, because he sure did a number on that leader's self-esteem. So what was the real reason this drummer wasn't wanted?

Growing Trend

In today's churches, the reason why we serve is being forgotten, or intentionally ignored. Many churches are trying to attract younger members, so they are getting rid of older people who are in highly visible roles, such as greeters, pastors, and MCs. Oh yeah, let's not forget about drummers. Yes. That's right. The church didn't care a bit about that drummer's playing because they were too distracted by the person's age and the effect it had on the image of the church. They had to get that person off the team some way without making it look suspicious.

They began by trying to beat down that person's confidence and pointing out things that were wrong with his or her playing, then they put the unsuspecting target into an improvement program, never to return. Now I have an interesting question. If that drummer was doing such a terrible job, then why were people coming from Connecticut, Rhode Island, and New Hampshire to see that drummer play *in church*? I know that to be true too, because I met some of those out-of-staters. I also heard that people from New York and Pennsylvania had inquired as well. And because that drummer had done some national touring, who knows where else the news could have been spreading to?

I don't know about you, but I would think that if a church is that concerned about building its membership, they would've embraced the opportunity to do just that. But instead, "they bit off their nose to spite their face." They could've used that person's popularity to attract people—not to mention having an old person who plays with more energy than almost any teenager, and has technical skills and hand speed not far behind that of Neil Peart. So, are you scratching your head yet? There are quite a few people in the music business as well as many members of that church who are.

There are two others I know of who were previously removed from a music team because of their age, and they were also not told the truth as to why. One of them was told he or she looked uncomfortable up there. I wouldn't be surprised if the church administrators are actually the ones who were uncomfortable with having older people on the platform. There are supposedly two others who are on the hit list as well.

Now what do you think about that? Does it sound right? Or just? Does it sound like something that Paul would have instructed the churches to do? Does it sound fair? Or is this age discrimination? What do you think God has to say about this?

"Stand up in the presence of the elderly, and show respect for the aged. Fear your God. I am the LORD.
—*Leviticus 19:32 (NLT)*

Never speak harshly to an older man, but appeal to him respectfully as you would to your own father ... Treat older women as you would your mother,
—*1 Timothy 5:1–2 (NLT)*

And the list goes on. Just look in any Bible.

I was recently talking to a friend from another church who told me about being placed in a similar program and then subsequently removed from the music team. This friend later found out through the grapevine that because of his or her age, he or she was no longer wanted on the team. This person also told me about another friend at yet another church who had the same thing happen. So as you can see, it has become very common in our Christian churches.

Hair that is turning white is like a crown of honor.
It is found in the way of being right with God.
—Proverbs 16:31 (NLV)

Brainwashed

I was having a conversation with a ministry leader about another leader who was disrespectful, dishonest, and condescending to me. And much to my surprise, this leader told me that I have to accept it and respect the other leader because he or she is a leader. Now I agree with respecting leaders. However, nobody, and I do mean *nobody,* should ever be expected to tolerate that kind of treatment from anybody. So in my response to that, I referred to Scripture that supports why we should never tolerate it. Even more to my surprise, this leader began explaining that the Scriptures don't apply to us because they are old pagan beliefs.

Now at this point, you could probably see the steam coming from my ears. I don't know where a true Christian would learn that kind of stuff, but it blatantly disagrees with the Bible. Period. Because if you want to call any of the letters of instructions from Paul and the other apostles to the churches pagan, then why are we reading the Bible to begin with? Those instructions applied then, and they most certainly do apply now. To believe otherwise has to be the result of false teaching or some kind of brainwashing, but it has no place in Christianity.

No, I imply that what pagans sacrifice they
offer to demons and not to God. I do not want
you to be participants with demons.
—1 Corinthians 10:20 (ESV)

Practice What You Preach

This old cliché rings so true in every walk of life—and, yes, even in our churches. How many times do we see church leaders giving us instructions to do things a certain way, only to turn around and do the exact opposite of what they tell us? That reminds me of another cliché: "Do as I say and not as I do."

A good example would be if we instruct our team members not to play or sing in a manner that could draw attention to themselves, and then we go out there ourselves, dance around, swing a guitar like a rock star would, and forget the lyrics—even though they're on the screen right in front of us. And, yes, I've seen it happen. Quite frequently, I might add.

> *They profess to know God, but in works they*
> *deny Him, being abominable, disobedient,*
> *and disqualified for every good work.*
> *—Titus 1:16 (NKJV)*

Dress Code

I've already touched on this a bit, but I'd like to reiterate and dig just a little deeper because this is extremely important when we're on the platform for the purpose of glorifying God's Kingdom. I did mention men wearing hats, and I know some of you may not like this. You may also disagree, but your argument isn't with me. It's with God. Yes, God. So like it or not, men are required to remove their hats in church, specifically in Christian churches. And 1 Corinthians 11 (NLT) spells this out quite clearly for us.

- Verse 4 says, "A man dishonors his head if he covers his head while praying or prophesying."

- Verse 7 says, "A man should not wear anything on his head when worshiping, for man is made in God's image and reflects God's glory."

I've had debates about this. And in every case, God has won that argument. You might say it's taken out of context. But is it? You may also try to say it's an old pagan belief. But come on now. You know you're just grasping at straws. And why? Because you want to wear a hat in church. Well, guess what. You can't. Period.

Those two verses are unquestionably clear, in or out of context. And don't ask why, but ask what. What do we all do in church? Do we not prophecy, pray, and worship? And what is First Corinthians? Is it not a letter of instructions from Paul to a Christian church?

My point is this: If we are on the platform representing God with the intent of glorifying His Kingdom, then we better be doing it in the most respectable way we possibly can, which brings me to this observation: torn clothing.

This doesn't seem to sit too well with a lot of people, so I definitely want to bring it to everybody's attention. My biblical understanding is that clothing was torn in an emotional response to grief, loss, or sin. It also signifies our separation from God. So my question for you is this: With that in mind, should we be allowed to wear ripped jeans or torn clothing on the platform? I'll give you the answer in a few minutes.

Then David took hold of his clothes and tore them, and so also did all the men who were with him. They mourned and wept and fasted until evening for Saul and his son Jonathan and for the people of the LORD and the house of Israel, because they had fallen by the sword.
—2 Samuel 1:11–12 (NASB)

Don't Lose Yourself

I knew a once well-liked church band leader whose name, since becoming the music team leader, has become the punch line of some not-so-funny jokes, none of which I care to repeat. It seemed as if this person had an overnight personality change, for the worse no less. That leader went from leading music shoulder to shoulder to leading the entire music team from on top of a pedestal, which seems to be getting taller by the day. And the sad thing is his or her fall is going to be much harder the higher up that pedestal goes. This isn't how any of us should lead God's music team. We are expected to lead by Jesus' good example, not Lucifer's poor example. So when we exalt ourselves, like Lucifer did, we'll end up being on a first-name basis with him.

The first thing we need to remember is that if we get called to be the leader of an entire music team, that doesn't make us a king or queen. It only means that our responsibilities as shepherds are now being expanded and the spotlights are getting brighter. So, in other words, we're now in a more visible role where we need to be much more careful about our behavior, the way we dress, and how we are treating others because everybody is watching us.

It's very unfortunate that not everybody gets this. As soon as some people become team leaders, they start behaving as though they've been given a license to be a psychological terrorist. Well, guess what. You can try that approach if you think that highly of yourself. But believe me, that fall from your pedestal is going to be extremely hard, and it will happen. The pastors will protect you for only so long. Because when somebody hurts enough people and the complaints begin piling up, there will be something done about it.

If we do well as band leaders and then someday are asked to lead the entire team, let's keep on doing what worked in our lesser roles because that's what got us elevated to team leader in the first place. There's no need to suddenly start acting like a boss or the king. Once we're there, we also mustn't allow ourselves to be intimidated by other team members who may be more experienced than we are. We need to embrace it so we ourselves can learn and grow.

Since God chose you to be the holy people he loves,
you must clothe yourselves with tenderhearted mercy,
kindness, humility, gentleness, and patience.
—*Colossians 3:12 (NLT)*

Be a Shepherd

How did Jesus lead His disciples? Was He on a pedestal? Was He on a throne? Or was He standing on a platform higher than all His faithful followers? No, no, and no. He was standing shoulder to shoulder with them. He was right down there in the thick of things, and he was dressed just like them. He sat in a boat at eye level. He sat in the grass or on a rock, but He never elevated Himself above anybody else. He is the King of all kings, and yet He never exalts Himself over us.

So then, why did His disciples follow Him? And why is it that we follow Him? Because He is our Shepherd. He is our Leader. He is our Ruler, but He rules by His leading and teaching. That's why we follow Him. He teaches us the rules. He guides us on our path. He heals our wounds and broken hearts. He poured out His blood for us so that we can be saved from our sins.

Jesus is the picture of a true Leader, a true King, a true Shepherd. That's how we should lead our music teams, or any ministry for that matter. We need to begin by setting the same kind of examples that Jesus Himself is setting. We need to put other people's needs before our own. Don't forget that everybody is looking at us and to us. They are learning by watching us, so we need to take our hats off in church. And don't forget, there's only one thing that should ever be torn in church: *the veil*, and not our clothing. Did you answer correctly?

Then, behold, the veil of the temple was torn in two from top to bottom; and the earth quaked, and the rocks were split,
—*Matthew 27:51 (NKJV)*

The Law

Whatever we do, the younger up-and-coming ministry leaders will copy, so we better be going by God's rules, by Jesus' teaching, by the Book. This can actually apply to any ministry. If we're serving God and preaching the Bible, it's in our best interest to be doing exactly what He says we should be doing. We can't just use whatever Scriptures or parts of Scriptures that fit our own personal preferences. We also can't omit whatever Scriptures we don't feel like obeying. If it's in the Bible, it's there for good reason, and we must follow it. Please remember the same laws that applied way back in the Old Testament applied in the New Testament, and they still apply today, tomorrow, and every day. The only thing that changed is the New Covenant replaced the Old Covenant. Jesus is now our High Priest. And He never said the old laws are obsolete.

God's laws should also be followed in every part of our lives. I've been hearing about a ministry leader who was abusive at home. Many of us are disappointed to hear that person has been allowed to remain in leadership. We are, however, thankful that the spouse had courage enough to get out of that situation. In 1

Timothy 3:4 (NASB), regarding appointment of overseers and deacons for the church at Ephesus, Paul says, "He must be one who manages his own household well". Shouldn't the same criteria also apply to our leaders of today's churches?

> *But the LORD said to Samuel, "Do not look at his*
> *appearance or at the height of his stature, because I have*
> *rejected him; for God sees not as man sees, for man looks at*
> *the outward appearance, but the LORD looks at the heart."*
> *—1 Samuel 16:7 (NASB)*

If we're part of a church that does preach the Bible, then our ministries and serving teams should all be following the same set of rules. We must be consistent, not only with each other, but also with Jesus. Because if we preach the Bible and then turn around and do our own thing that doesn't agree with the Bible, isn't that a little like New Age thinking?

> *You younger men, likewise, be subject to your elders;*
> *and all of you, clothe yourselves with humility*
> *toward one another, for GOD IS OPPOSED TO THE*
> *PROUD, BUT GIVES GRACE TO THE HUMBLE.*
> *—1 Peter 5:5 (NASB)*

Stop pretending that you've never been bad
You're never wrong and you've never been dirty
You're such a saint, that ain't the way we see you
—Alice Cooper

CHAPTER 12

The Bottom Line

as it is written: "None is righteous, no, not one; no one
understands, no one seeks for God. All have turned aside,
together they have gone wrong; no one does good, not
even one." "Their throat is an open grave, they use their
tongues to deceive." "The venom of asps is under their
lips." Their mouth is full of curses and bitterness." "Their
feet are swift to shed blood, in their paths are ruin and
misery, and the way of peace they do not know." "There
is no fear of God before their eyes." Now we know that
whatever the law says it speaks to those who are under
the law, so that every mouth may be stopped, and the
whole world may be held accountable to God. For no
human being will be justified in his sight by works of the
law, since through the law comes knowledge of sin.
—Romans 3:10–20 (RSV)

It's really sad how image conscience our society has become.
We care so much about how we look to others that we're willing
to go into debt over it. We drive cars we can't afford. But that
doesn't matter as long we impress others. We receive daily

reminders of our foolishness too. The bills in the mail. And how do we handle it? We keep falling behind and never seem to catch up. Why? Because the next thing comes along that we absolutely have to have.

> *Vanity of vanities, saith the Preacher, vanity of*
> *vanities; all is vanity. What profit hath a man of*
> *all his labour which he taketh under the sun?*
> —*Ecclesiastes 1:2–3 (KJV)*

The saddest part is that our modern churches are just as image conscience as we are. They'll go as far as getting rid of the older members of the serving team regardless of their skills, just to put young, pretty people in the high-visibility roles regardless of their lack of skills. Now I may have missed it, but I don't recall reading in the Bible that only younger, good-looking people are allowed to serve God. We go to church and listen to great messages straight from the Bible, but are the preachers practicing what they're preaching? When you come right down to it, you need to ask yourself, "Is the modern church actually serving God? Is it still a church? Or has it become a business?"

> *Yet I am not surprised! Satan can change himself into*
> *an angel of light, so it is no wonder his servants can do*
> *it too, and seem like godly ministers. In the end they will*
> *get every bit of punishment their wicked deeds deserve.*
> —*2 Corinthians 11:14–15 (TLB)*

Status Quo

One thing I have observed, which bothers me a bit, is how people act as though serving is some sort of status symbol. And before I go on, I want to point out that I'm also guilty of this, which could account for why it bothers me. The more we do, the higher our status gets in our own minds. We rate our success as Christians by how much serving we do, how much praying we do, and how often we attend church service.

"So when you give to the poor, do not sound a trumpet before you, as the hypocrites do in the synagogues and in the streets, so that they may be honored by men. Truly I say to you, they have their reward in full.
—*Matthew 6:2 (NASB)*

We work to become more prestigious by achieving leadership roles and continue climbing. And once we do achieve our target roles, we believe that we're more important than others, so we begin treating them like they are beneath us. Now is that how God instructs us to treat each other? Is that the way you would like to be treated by your Christian brothers and sisters?

Think of the kindness you wish others would show you; do the same for them.
—*Luke 6:31 (VOICE)*

Worship Team

In a lot of churches, the band, choir, or music ensemble is called the worship team. Music, as important as it is, however, is only a small part of true worship. All other aspects of church service contribute to worship just as much as music, if not more. So now with that in mind, why isn't the parking ministry called the worship team? Or the greeters? Or the ushers? I think you get the point. They are all part of the worship team. The church's serving team is the worship team. The Bible makes this point quite evident.

In his book *Biblical Worship—Pursuing Intimacy with God*, Dr. Greg McCabe says, "Worship is a way of life," and he delves into the nitty-gritty of how God, Jesus, Paul, and others instruct us to worship correctly. Until I read his book, I used to view music as being the worship portion of church service. I strongly recommend this book for all church leaders and congregants. It's a real eye-opener.

At the church I'm now a member of, I am the chair-man of our worship team. I go in early Sunday morning to set up and disinfect the chairs, along with whatever else needs to be set up. But with all joking aside, that is what I do. I worship God by setting up chairs.

"It's who you are and the way you live that count before God. Your worship must engage your spirit in the pursuit of truth. That's the kind of people the Father is out looking for: those who are simply and honestly themselves before Him in their worship. God is sheer being itself— Spirit. Those who worship him must do it out of their very being, their spirits, their true selves, in adoration."
—John 4:23–24 (MSG)

Bad Business

What does the Bible say a church should be? I'm pretty sure Jesus said His Father's house is a place of worship and prayer, and that everyone is welcome. And with what I see with the phasing out of older people and replacing them with young, pretty people, it seems like there's more emphasis on the church's image than on worship. Maybe it's just me, but doesn't that resemble marketing?

I once heard somebody say something along these lines:

"Tell them whatever it takes to get them here. Tell them there are pretty women if you have to. Just get them here." Does that sound like a good Christian thing to say? Or more like a sales pitch, maybe?

> *He said to them, "The Scriptures declare,*
> *'My Temple will be a house of prayer,' but you*
> *have turned it into a den of thieves."*
> *—Luke 19:46 (NLT)*

So once I research this a little further, maybe I'll be able to put together enough material for my next book in this series: *Be a Pastor Not a Salesman.* Badum psh. Where's there a drummer when you need one? Yeah, I'm kidding again, but it is something we should all be more aware of.

Please don't get me wrong though, because I have been blessed to be mentored and coached by some really awesome church leaders who are the real deal. But I've also been patronized, stabbed in the back, and lied to by people pretending to be my friends.

> *When he speaks graciously, do not believe him,*
> *For there are seven abominations in his heart.*
> *—Proverbs 26:25 (NASB)*

So when you're leading a ministry in a church, no matter what denomination, you need to take into consideration what they are following—the Bible or marketing strategies? If it's the latter, then you may want to consider going to a different church. Because if they're not following or living up to the standards of the Bible, what's their true motive?

"No one can serve two masters. Either you
will hate the one and love the other, or you will
be devoted to the one and despise the other.
You cannot serve both God and money.
—Matthew 6:24 (NIV)

The Bottom Line

As I mentioned in the third chapter, bullies come in all shapes and sizes. And since bullying in itself is true evil, it only stands to reason that evil in general comes in all shapes and sizes. And as I also alluded to, with my own words and with Scripture and quotes, it's not at all uncommon for Satan and his demons to infiltrate our churches under the guise of church leaders. It happens more often than we'd care to admit and closer to home as well.

However, this doesn't mean that just because a person isn't a very good leader that he or she should be automatically labeled as evil. It could just be a simple lack of experience, maturity or understanding on his or her part. And if we find ourselves falling into this category, we need to admit it and seek help so that we can become worthy leaders.

Being a leader also doesn't mean that we just start bossing people around, although it does give us authority to do so. It means that we'll be looked up to as role models, so we need to be setting the best possible examples as Christians that we can. It also means that we must be practicing exactly—and, yes, I do mean *exactly*—what we preach. So if we're preaching the Bible, we need to be practicing the Bible, and not just talking a good game.

I apologize for repeating myself, but edifying others is a very important aspect of being a true leader. And admitting when we're wrong or don't know something is also very important, because nobody likes a know-it-all, especially when he or she doesn't know.

And if you're all about telling others what to do and how to do it instead of helping them to improve in a productive, respectful way, then you're in the wrong business. Because the business Jesus is in is all about helping, healing, and edifying others. So remember, He took His ragtag bunch of misfits and made them all feel important. He then sent them out into this cruel world to build His church, and they did. And it's still standing.

The bottom line is this: Be a shepherd not a king, a leader not a ruler.

shepherd the flock of God among you, exercising oversight not under compulsion, but voluntarily, according to the will of God; and not for sordid gain, but with eagerness; nor yet as lording it over those allotted to your charge, but proving to be examples to the flock.
—1 Peter 5:2–3 (NASB)

Red-Handed

In 1971, Carly Simon wrote a song titled "You're So Vain." The lyrics of the chorus go something like this: "You're so vain. You probably think this song is about you. Don't you?"

So with that being said, there are probably some people who think this book is about them. In fact, they could be reading it right now. But if you notice, I was careful not to use anybody's actual name. I don't like pointing fingers or badmouthing people. I would prefer to protect them rather than to call negative attention to them.

> *But I say to you, love your enemies, bless those who*
> *curse you, do good to those who hate you, and pray*
> *for those who spitefully use you and persecute you,*
> *—Matthew 5:44 (NKJV)*

If you do think this book is about you, yet deny anything that was mentioned, then it can't possibly be about you. Can it? But if you have done or thought about doing anything that was mentioned, then it could be about you. It could be about me. It could be about any of us. Guilt does have a way of catching up with us though. Doesn't it?

> *...and you may be sure that your sin will find you out.*
> *—Numbers 32:23 (NIV)*

So if I may paraphrase a bit, "You're so vain. You probably think this *book* is about you. Don't you?" Well, it's in God's hands now, and He knows the truth. I have no authority to pass judgment, and neither does anyone else, except for God. But if I were to make an educated guess based on what I've seen, experienced and researched, I would tend to believe that there are quite a few church leaders who should probably be getting their asbestos suits ready.

> *The eyes of the LORD are in every place,*
> *Watching the evil and the good.*
> *—Proverbs 15:3 (NASB)*

> *Evil plans are an abomination to the LORD,*
> *But pleasant words are pure.*
> *—Proverbs 15:26 (NASB)*

For if anyone thinks he is something when
he is nothing, he deceives himself.
—*Galatians 6:3 (NASB)*

When you and I choose not to align our actions
with God's truth—when we live in blatant rebellion
against His will for us—we leave our heart
exposed where Satan can take a clear shot.
—Priscilla Shirer

Soliloquy

LORD, how are they increased that trouble me!
many are they that rise up against me.
—*Psalm 3:1 (KJV)*

They cry out for help, only to fall on deaf ears. And when we do finally listen, it's usually too late. For they have fallen victim to the very ones they believed were supposed to protect them. The wolf comes in many disguises. He wears king's clothing and fools only himself. He wears sheep's clothing and fools the sheep and sometimes the shepherd. He wears shepherd's clothing and fools everybody, except for one, the one who cried out.

O God of my praise, Do not be silent! For they have opened the wicked and deceitful mouth against me; They have spoken against me with a lying tongue. They have also surrounded me with words of hatred, And fought against me without cause. In return for my love they act as my accusers; But I am in prayer. Thus they have repaid me evil for good And hatred for my love. Appoint a wicked man over him, And let an accuser stand at his right hand. When he is judged, let him come forth guilty, And let his prayer become sin. Let his days be few; Let another take his office.
—*Psalm 109:1–8 (NASB)*

When someone betrays or turns against us, God instructs us not to seek revenge, but to seek His face in prayer. He knows best how to deal with the situation, and we need to hear from Him.
—Charles F. Stanley

Conclusion

Here I am a year and a half later, completing the arduous task of writing my first book and hopefully not my last. The coronavirus is upon us, and nobody is certain when this horrible thing will come to an end. So if you have a copy of this book in your hand, you know that the enemy didn't prevent me from finishing it. You've been blessed as well to make it through the nightmare.

In writing this book, my intention was not as much about showing how to lead as how not to lead. These assessments are based on my personal experiences and many of my own mistakes that I've made as a leader along with some observations I've made of other leaders. I also spoke with people from several churches—pastors, churchgoers, band members, and leaders—and there does seem to be quite a bit of agreement with my views, especially when it comes to who is following the Bible and who isn't.

There are also going to be people who don't agree, and that's OK. For those who don't, I would suggest asking yourself why you don't agree. Perhaps you're afraid of what you will see when you look in the mirror. Or you may simply choose to ignore the Bible altogether because you think you have it all figured out. If I may make a suggestion, it would be to look in the mirror, read the Bible, and then begin to follow it. You never know. Your attitude toward God just may begin to change.

Now before we close this book, I'd like to draw your attention to Proverbs 3:5–6 (MSG) one more time.

Trust God from the bottom of your heart; don't try
to figure out everything on your own. Listen for
God's voice in everything you do, everywhere you
go. He's the One who will keep you on track.

I do so because these verses really speak to me and I have found them to be foundational for the writing of this book. I also find them to be foundational for every aspect of our daily lives, especially in our walk with God. And if they're not, they should be.

You may have noticed that I used these verses multiple times throughout this book with different translations. That was quite intentional on my part. I did so in an effort to prompt you to meditate on them and plant them on your heart. I really can't stress strongly enough how important these verses are. In fact, I could possibly have added a whole chapter dedicated to them alone. However, I do believe as long as you keep them firmly in your heart, situations will arise where you will be glad that you did.

I repeated other verses as well, also in different translations for the same reason. I believe there's no such thing as too much repetition when it comes to reading the Bible.

I also want to point out again just how important it is to humble ourselves and swallow our pride. I know there may be leaders out there who won't like this. And not too many years ago, I would've been one of them. I'll also admit that I still catch myself being haughty every now and then. I'm a work in progress though, just like anybody else.

Pride is a nasty characteristic. And as Charles F. Stanley

puts it, "God puts pride in the same category with murder!" Pride, according to the Bible, is one of the seven deadly sins. Yes, pride is a sin, like it or not, and God hates it. I know *hate* is a strong and negative word, but it's true. He hates pride—as stated in Proverbs 16:5 (NLT), "The LORD detests the proud; they will surely be punished."

Pride can and will prevent us from being the shepherds that God wants us to be. It gives the enemy an opening. And from there, we become bullies, so let's not let pride become a part of us. Let's be shepherds, not kings.

> *But He gives a greater grace. Therefore it says,*
> *"GOD IS OPPOSED TO THE PROUD, BUT*
> *GIVES GRACE TO THE HUMBLE."*
> *—James 4:6 (NASB)*

Thank you for taking the time to read this book. I truly hope you enjoyed it. But most importantly, I hope you got something out of it. I don't claim to know it all. But I have seen the expressions on enough people's faces to help me to learn from my own mistakes. So always remember, the eyes don't lie.

> *But now indeed there are many members, yet one body. And the eye cannot say to the hand, "I have no need of you"; nor again the head to the feet, "I have no need of you." No, much rather, those members of the body which seem to be weaker are necessary. And those members of the body which we think to be less honorable, on these we bestow greater honor; and our unpresentable parts have greater modesty, but our presentable parts have no need. But God composed the body, having given greater honor to that part which lacks it, that there should be no schism in the body, but that the*

members should have the same care for one another. And
if one member suffers, all the members suffer with it; or if
one member is honored, all the members rejoice with it.
—*1 Corinthians 12:20–26 (NKJV)*

Leaders will be judged, and we will be judged.
Leaders will be judged for their decisions, and
their judgement will be more severe than ours.
—John Bevere

Let us close in prayer.

Dear God, Heavenly Father,
You have called us to be shepherds, not kings.
Thank you for trusting us with Your flock.
Please forgive us for our pride and help us to be humble.
Give us the wisdom, the discernment, the love,
and the understanding it takes to be true shepherds.
Please, God, give us the ability to recognize when
we're wrong, and the courage to admit it.
Let us not be self-exalting, but instead, may we edify others.
Please, God, open our minds, our eyes, our ears, and our hearts
so that we can embrace the advice and input of others.
Let us be friendly and peaceful, not pushy and bossy.
Help us to remember that we too are part of Your team.
Please, God, help us to follow Your Living Example.
Give us the heart and mind of Jesus, the True Shepherd.
Please guide us to be leaders, not rulers.
To be shepherds, not kings.
In Jesus' name, amen.

Bible Translation Guide

Some of you may not be familiar with the many different translations available for the Holy Bible. Not only has it been translated in many languages, but it has also been translated into many English versions, some of which you have seen throughout this book.

There are many more available than this, but here is a list of the translations I used in the writing of this book. I hope you find this to be helpful.

Amplified Bible (AMP)
Complete Jewish Bible (CJB)
Contemporary English Version (CEV)
Easy-to-Read Version (ERV)
English Standard Version (ESV)
Good News Translation (GNT)
International Standard Version (ISV)
King James Version (KJV)
The Message (MSG)
Modern English Version (MEV)
New American Standard Bible (NASB)
New International Reader's Version (NIRV)
New International Version (NIV)
New King James Version (NKJV)
New Life Version (NLV)
New Living Translation (NLT)

Revised Standard Version (RSV)
The Living Bible (TLB)
The Voice (VOICE)
World English Bible (WEB)

> *Therefore the name of the city was Babel—because*
> *there the Lord confused the language of the entire*
> *earth; and from that place the Lord scattered and*
> *dispersed them over the surface of all the earth.*
> *—Genesis 11:9 (AMP)*

Suggested Reading

There are so many great books I could recommend, but that could possibly make up at least half of a chapter. So here are some of the great ones that I found myself reading multiple times. It would also be difficult for me to put them in order of preference, except of course the first one. I have mentioned a few of these throughout this book, and I included some other favorites of mine. I'm pretty sure you'll find them to be quite helpful, especially the first one.

The Holy Bible (The Charles F. Stanley Life Principles Bible)
God

The Core of Christianity
Dr. Neil T. Anderson

Biblical Worship—Pursuing Intimacy with God
Dr. Greg McCabe

The Holy Spirit—Activating God's Power in Your Life
Billy Graham

The Grace Awakening
Charles R. Swindoll

Secrets of a Prayer Warrior
Derek Prince

The Armor of God (Bible study)
Priscilla Shirer

The Pilgrim's Progress
John Bunyan

The Case for Christ
Lee Strobel

Battlefield of the Mind—Devotional
Joyce Meyer

The Purpose Driven Life
Rick Warren

The Problem of God
Mark Clark

Hope for Each Day—Devotional
Billy Graham

The Practice of the Presence of God
Brother Lawrence

Victory over the Darkness
Dr. Neil T. Anderson

Walk with God—Devotional
Chris Tiegreen

The God You May Not Know
David Jeremiah

The Gospel in Brief
Leo Tolstoy

A Praying Life—Connecting with God in a Distracting World
Paul E. Miller

> *Jesus did many other things as well. If every one of them*
> *were written down, I suppose that even the whole world*
> *would not have room for the books that would be written.*
> *—John 21:25 (NIV)*

Printed in the United States
by Baker & Taylor Publisher Services